AF269975

SMALL
but

# SMALL but 

## How Everyday Habits Add Up to More Manageable and Confident Teaching

## MIRIAM PLOTINSKY

Arlington, Virginia USA

 **ascd**

2800 Shirlington Road, Suite 1001 • Arlington, VA 22206 USA
Phone: 800-933-2723 or 703-578-9600
Website: www.ascd.org • Email: member@ascd.org
Author guidelines: www.ascd.org/write

Richard Culatta, *Chief Executive Officer;* Anthony Rebora, *Chief Content Officer;* Genny Ostertag, *Managing Director, Book Acquisitions & Editing;* Susan Hills, *Senior Acquisitions Editor;* Mary Beth Nielsen, *Director, Book Editing;* Miriam Calderone, *Editor;* Lisa Hill, *Graphic Designer;* Cynthia Stock, *Typesetter;* Kelly Marshall, *Production Manager;* Shajuan Martin, *E-Publishing Specialist;* Kathryn Oliver, *Creative Project Manager*

Copyright © 2024 ASCD. All rights reserved. It is illegal to reproduce copies of this work in print or electronic format (including reproductions displayed on a secure intranet or stored in a retrieval system or other electronic storage device from which copies can be made or displayed) without the prior written permission of the publisher. By purchasing only authorized electronic or print editions and not participating in or encouraging piracy of copyrighted materials, you support the rights of authors and publishers. Readers who wish to reproduce or republish excerpts of this work in print or electronic format may do so for a small fee by contacting the Copyright Clearance Center (CCC), 222 Rosewood Dr., Danvers, MA 01923, USA (phone: 978-750-8400; fax: 978-646-8600; web: www.copyright.com). To inquire about site licensing options or any other reuse, contact ASCD Permissions at www.ascd.org/permissions or permissions@ascd.org. For a list of vendors authorized to license ASCD ebooks to institutions, see www.ascd.org/epubs. Send translation inquiries to translations@ascd.org.

ASCD® is a registered trademark of Association for Supervision and Curriculum Development. All other trademarks contained in this book are the property of, and reserved by, their respective owners, and are used for editorial and informational purposes only. No such use should be construed to imply sponsorship or endorsement of the book by the respective owners.

All web links in this book are correct as of the publication date below but may have become inactive or otherwise modified since that time. If you notice a deactivated or changed link, please email books@ascd.org with the words "Link Update" in the subject line. In your message, please specify the web link, the book title, and the page number on which the link appears.

PAPERBACK ISBN: 978-1-4166-3315-0   ASCD product #125003                 n9/24
PDF EBOOK ISBN: 978-1-4166-3316-7; see Books in Print for other formats.
Quantity discounts are available: email programteam@ascd.org or call 800-933-2723, ext. 5773, or 703-575-5773. For desk copies, go to www.ascd.org/deskcopy.

Library of Congress Cataloging-in-Publication Data is available for this title.
LCCN: 2024029813

33 32 31 30 29 28 27 26 25 24          1 2 3 4 5 6 7 8 9 10 11 12

*To the countless exemplary teachers who have given me
small but mighty tips over the years:
I thank you.*

*To my father, who was my biggest cheerleader:
I miss you.*

*To Kenny, who is my happy place:
I love you.*

SMALL
but
MIGHTY

# Acknowledgments

In May 2020—two months into the pandemic shutdown, when life was uncertain and unfamiliar—I got an email from a senior acquisitions editor at ASCD asking me if I'd ever thought about writing a book. Four books later, we have finally been able to work together. Susan Hills, thank you for finding me, for being a discerning editor with a keen eye for the details I miss, and for being such a champion of my work. Also, many thanks to everyone at ASCD who worked so hard to make this book a reality, especially Miriam Calderone.

My writing career has continued to grow with help from editors who believe in me. For that, I owe a huge debt of gratitude to Carol Chambers Collins, Tom Berger, and Kelly Clancy.

For the past 24 years, I have been fortunate to work in a school district with dedicated, talented educators. To all my teammates, past and present, you inspire me and make me better.

Whenever I need to learn more about social-emotional learning, my go-to experts are Alex Shevrin Venet and Phyllis Fagell. You are both so supportive, not to mention ceaselessly generous with your time and ideas. Thank you for always being willing to help me put things in perspective.

To the Plotinsky crew, I'm glad we are both geographically and emotionally close. I continue to learn from my mother, who is a model of persistence and courage. Only the strongest people are resilient enough to keep embracing new experiences, and I'm so proud to have a mom who has taught me by example.

Not every education writer is lucky enough to have three supportive kids who come to local book events and get excited when each new book is published. Even better, they are all a lot of fun, especially now that we've solidly hit the adolescent years. Koby, Ayla, and Dalya: keep being your distinct, incomparable selves, and thank you for patiently teaching me about this whole motherhood thing. I'm still working on getting it down pat.

Kenny, I hope you don't mind that I keep dedicating books to you. But how can I help it? Nearly 20 years in, you are still the best thing that ever happened to me, and I don't expect that to ever change. Thanks for the coffee, for walking our fourth child at crazy hours (and driving the other three around), for keeping it all going, and for loving me, just the way I am.

# Introduction: Why Small but Mighty?

"You look so Zen," my colleague said as she walked up to me.

It was a beautiful spring day, one of those rare gifts when the sky is pure blue, the sun shines, and a gentle breeze ruffles budding blossoms. My colleague was headed to her car to grab something she had left behind, and I was using a 15-minute break to get some fresh air, eat an apple, and clear my head.

At her comment, I laughed. "Trust me, I'm not."

"No, really," she insisted. "You always seem to keep calm, even when everyone around us might be losing it. Is that something you do on purpose?"

As I paused to think about her question, I couldn't help but reflect on the hard work it took to keep things in perspective. At that point I was about 20 years into my career and was hitting the highest threshold of stress I'd ever experienced. Multiple factors played into that, but to condense them all, I had too many jobs to complete with not enough time. The term *bandwidth* was not yet in general use to describe any given person's capacity to accomplish something, but mine was stretched incredibly thin. My colleague might have thought that I was handling it all, but I was barely hanging on.

There may be no formal studies to capture the proclivities of people who decide to become educators, but I would guess that most teachers probably lean more toward Type A than Type B personalities. It's hard to be laid-back when so many moving parts are in play at once:

skillful lesson planning (often for multiple classes), effective instruction, thoughtful analysis of and reflection on student progress, and the ability to change course when things aren't working. Add to that the constant demands on time and wellness, and it can become overwhelming to manage a job that is highly unpredictable and changes from moment to moment. Even people who tend to be flexible can wind up succumbing to the multiple stressors that emerge in school buildings.

It's important to keep an eye on the big picture of what matters most, especially when we consider where students need to wind up with their learning and what it will take to accomplish that growth. However, the tiny details of how we get there are just as vital a consideration. In classroom teaching, no detail is insignificant. Skillful teachers are highly attuned to the importance of reflective practice and how it affects their ability to teach similar content each year while making needed adjustments to instructional approaches that maximize student achievement. How is it possible to increase awareness of the small but mighty details that have a big impact on student growth?

When we embrace the details of instruction with an approach that builds capacity over time, both teachers and students reap the benefits of *habits* over *motivation*. Many educators consider intrinsic motivation to be the gold standard for achievement, but it can be transient even in the most devoted people. That is why the small things we do every day by rote become our salvation during a rough patch or when we can't find enough mental energy for inspiration. Students with strong habits produce good results even when they're having a hard time, and the same holds true for adults.

When my colleague observed what she called "Zen" behavior in my outward appearance, I was initially surprised. After all, my internal monologue wasn't nearly as relaxed at that time in my life as I would have wanted it to be. However, upon reflection, I realized that I was in the habit of doing tiny things each day to mitigate that high stress load. Getting outside for just a little bit of time was a big help, as it reminded me of the world beyond cinder block walls. I was insistent about having the first hour of the morning to myself to orient the day, drink my coffee, and get organized before colleagues and students arrived. At the end of the day, I turned off my phone an hour before bed and spent time with my family. Taken alone, these moves were nearly infinitesimal in their application, but together, they made living a more fulfilled personal and professional life possible.

As nearly every teacher knows, achieving longevity in education is about embracing both the successes and the obstacles we encounter as part of a journey to growth. Teaching is a marathon rife with unpredictability and demand, and without much staying power. According to a *Vox* report, "Beginning teachers have among the highest rates of turnover of any group of teachers. Overall, more than 44 percent of new teachers leave the profession within five years" (Cineas, 2022). To make it in the field of education past the time that so many teachers throw in the towel, it's essential to lean into the details that add up to success.

The upcoming chapters explore a variety of moves and tools that may seem bite-sized and therefore insignificant on their own, but yield great power when implemented systematically and thoughtfully. To get a better sense of why small equals mighty, let's look at some of the theories that demonstrate the subtle influence of habits, brevity, and the wise advice that less is more.

## Habit Stacking

In his bestselling book *Atomic Habits,* author James Clear (2018) writes, "It is so easy to overestimate the importance of one defining moment and underestimate the value of making small improvements on a daily basis" (p. 15). This appropriately bite-sized statement aptly summarizes the idea behind the practice known as "habit stacking," which involves layering small habits on top of one another, one at a time, to produce enduring results.

In education, teachers place a lot of understandable emphasis on finding effective ways to motivate students. Extrinsic motivators such as grades and reward systems do not generally have a profound or lasting impact on performance, and many students are not at all moved by such measures, even in the shorter term. Therefore, the phrase "intrinsic motivation" has come to express a coveted goal in teaching as we search for the key to unlocking a deeper sense of value for learning in our students.

The problem is that even when teachers discover how to access intrinsic drive in students, it can be just as transient as extrinsic motivation. Suppose, for example, that a student is truly interested in becoming a better writer because she wants to be a journalist. Historically, she is high-performing and engaged in class. However, because of various life stressors and obstacles, she has become discouraged and begins to lag in her schoolwork, including her writing assignments. Her teachers observe this change and try to encourage her to recover her drive, but they are otherwise at a loss about what to do.

This kind of situation is precisely where habits outdo motivation and are therefore a far more useful avenue to explore in teaching and learning. As Clear (2018) points out, "You do not rise to the level of your goals. You fall to the level of your systems" (p. 27). When we continuously rely on motivation to succeed, we are setting ourselves up for failure because it is too unreliable a factor in ultimate success. However, when we build careful habits over time, they become nearly automatic and are therefore much more effective.

To illustrate this idea, consider a parent who wants to instill healthier eating habits in his children. Removing all processed snack foods overnight will likely result in an uprising, and no change will occur. However, a more measured approach could achieve this parent's goals gradually and effectively. Perhaps for one week, he might experiment with putting a fruit and vegetable plate on the table for the kids to snack on as he subtly drags his feet to get dinner on the table. With ready access to a choice of fresh produce, the children are likely to start picking at the plate within that first week. Then, the parent might put healthier snack choices in places within easy sight and reach of smaller bodies and push the less ideal choices a bit further out of the way. The subtle friction that occurs from the change in access would help the children automatically select whatever is more easily available. As the weeks progress, this parent can continue to layer on similar moves to change his children's dietary habits in ways that are as intentional as they are lasting.

In education, a similar approach yields equally desired results. In the earlier example of the writing student who lost her motivation, she might be able to continue producing work if her teacher has implemented daily writing routines that do not require inspiration or even too much brain power. Instead, the goal behind such habits would be to write anything at all, with editing occurring later. With this "low floor, high ceiling" approach, students begin in accessible places and then move up toward the expected higher standard rather than constantly feeling as though they must do their best immediately and on demand.

With habit stacking, small and mighty overrides big shifts in behavior. Clear (2018) affirms, "Too often, we convince ourselves that massive success requires massive action" (p. 15). Instead, it is the smaller, daily habits that we engage in without much thought that produce desired results. Throughout this book, tools and strategies are shared that embrace this bite-sized approach to reaching the goal of consistent success with students. More than huge moves that are likely to cause disruption rather than meaningful change, the tiny details that influence teaching and learning have far greater importance and impact.

## Brevity

Nearly every day, many people feel like they're drowning in a rising tide of too much information. Thanks to the ubiquitous presence of connectivity via smartphones, smartwatches, and other forms of technology, life is dominated by the constant inundation of news, communications, and tasks. It's no wonder that health and wellness experts recommend that people limit time with devices and screens, and it's equally understandable that it's a struggle to let go of the addictive accessibility.

In addition to the mental fatigue that results from constantly being in the loop, teachers deal with another layer of exhaustion: the fact that at work, being in front of students requires mentally or physically (and often both) keeping our brains and bodies set to the "on" switch. That is why, when new district or school initiatives are laid out in front of teaching staff, no matter how helpful or valid they may be, the first reaction is almost always a jaded "Please don't give us another thing to do."

As author and marketing expert Joseph McCormack (2014) writes in *Brief: Make a Bigger Impact by Saying Less,* "The new brutal reality is that people are drowning in information. It floods them everywhere they go" (p. 14). If leaders do not step up and become more aware of this problem, McCormack argues, they will not be able to help their employees maintain focus on the most important priorities. Therefore, he says, change depends on action: "You have to put it in a smaller package and make it easier to consume and digest. You must boil it down and get to the point quickly, or be forgotten" (p. 22).

For educators, actively practicing brevity can be challenging. So much pressure exists to "cover" a curriculum, creating the false impression that speed is more important than depth of understanding. Furthermore, every school day includes unpredictable situations that have to be quickly processed and handled, ideally in order of urgency and importance. When so much is flying at a person's head at once, figuring out how to get to the point feels like a nice idea that cannot possibly work in reality.

However, for the sake of both learning and well-being, taking a pause in all but the most dire situations is a habit that leads to more effective practice. Suppose that on a challenging day with students, a mental to-do list keeps threatening a teacher's inner sense of calm with the despairing thought that nothing can be accomplished within the ideal time frame. In such instances, it is worth taking a few minutes after class to write out the list items that are most worrisome and then put a star next to the ones that are truly urgent. In most cases, it may feel uncomfortable to push many actions on that list to another time, but not impossible. Getting to the point of what needs to be done creates a far more tenable situation. In the rare event that all the items are still somehow urgent, then deeper questions must be asked about how much work is being externally imposed upon the teacher and how much involves a more intrinsic level of choice and a potential need to change behavior.

Ultimately, cutting down the scope of practice on any given day has the opposite effect of what people assume will happen. Rather than making anyone less attentive or aware, applying more focus to fewer tasks creates a heightened level of efficacy. Just as weightlifters benefit more from completing five challenging bicep curls than by pushing too far, injuring themselves and ruining their form by doing 10 repetitions, embracing less to accomplish more holds great value in classrooms, for both teacher pedagogy and student growth.

# Less Is More

"I'm never going to get through this," my friend said to me one day as we sat at a table together, grading papers.

"What's that?" I asked him.

In response, he showed me something I'd seen before and been privately concerned about: a to-do list that stretched several notebook pages long, marked up with asterisks and crowded notes in the margin. "It's impossible," he said, stating what was obvious. "I have at least 200 essays sitting on my desk right now that I collected weeks ago, and there are so many other assignments I'm also trying to grade. There's no way to catch up."

I wasn't sure if my colleague was asking for advice or just venting, but his frustration level was high enough that I wanted to help. "How many assignments do you typically give students each week?" I asked.

Without a word, he turned his laptop around so that I could see the student gradebook. As I looked, I thought at first that my eyes were deceiving me. We were only three weeks into the quarter, but there were enough entries on the screen to represent an entire marking period's worth of work. "How many assignments is that?" I asked.

"Let me see," he said, squinting. "Looks like 36 in total. And I've only graded about half of those, maybe a little less. Lots of blank spots in there."

Leaning in, I tried to get a firmer understanding of what was represented in the gradebook. "So you have some quizzes, a bunch of small activities, three essays, and two projects. What are the rest of these? What does 'GMP' stand for?"

"Oh," he said, "that's grammar and mechanics practice. We do those every day, just for a few minutes at the start of class."

"And you grade every single one?"

"That's the idea," he said. "I'm not saying it happens."

"The way I look at it, teaching is overwhelming enough. We don't need to up the ante. In my mind, it's not about the number of assignments we give or how many we grade. It's about how kids are spending their time. Depth over breadth."

"I get that concept," he said, "but I've never understood what it looks like in reality."

Looking at his pile of papers, his to-do list, and the gradebook once more, it dawned on me that to tell my friend to just stop doing so much was never going to be feasible. Instead, he would need to take some baby steps toward getting more out of doing less.

"Do you want suggestions?" I asked. "Or maybe you want me to drop it? Either is fine; I promise I won't be offended."

"No, please," he said, "I'll take any advice."

"Maybe you can start small with just one little action. What gives you the most stress?"

Without hesitation he said, "My grading, definitely."

"OK," I said, "then the priority should be to get it more under control. Can you divide the pile into things that have to be graded without delay and assignments that might be able to wait or that are more expendable?"

"Maybe," he said, "but I would feel bad about that. The kids gave me their work with the expectation that I would grade it."

"Totally get it, but is it possible that trying to get it all done in a rush is doing them a disservice, rather than taking time to grade what's really important with more time and care?"

He tilted his head to one side, considering. "I don't know."

"Generally," I said, "kids aren't so much into us grading a ton of work. It's more that they want quick and clear feedback so that they can do well. We can't assess that way if we're overworked."

"OK, I'm listening. So, how do I grade less?"

"Let's start by making some piles," I said, pointing at the stack.

To make a long story short, my friend and I worked for several months on gradually paring down his grading, from assigning less (a big challenge for someone who was used to partially using grading as a behavior management technique) to being more intentional about which assignments would be given only feedback and which would also include grades. At first it was difficult for him to let go of the habits that were trapping him in a ceaseless treadmill of work, but once he started seeing the benefits of another way, he was sold on the change.

As McCormack (2014) shares, "When you are throwing things out, it may be hard to decide what goes—but keep in mind what people will really care about" (p. 36). Helping my friend manage a grading pile that had gotten far out of hand involved some difficult decisions. However, starting the ball rolling by doing less to achieve more saved his sanity—and perhaps his longevity in teaching. Similarly, teachers who seek to be effective at a demanding job that undergoes constant shifts must become comfortable with agility. Being nimble with instructional practice is an essential step in determining what is serving students and ourselves, and what might need to be jettisoned.

Habit stacking, brevity, and the idea that less is more all add up to one bigger idea: small actions are mighty, and they produce results. In teaching, the details matter. To that end, the coming chapters are filled with strategies for applying small and mighty moves to teaching practice before, during, and after instruction, as well as the spaces in between when well-being and belonging become paramount to long-term success. Every figure and tool is designed for immediate, practical application in the classroom.

To get the most out of this book, listening to your inner teaching voice is paramount. Certain ideas will fit more naturally into your existing practice, whereas others require more of a stretch. Starting with what is more familiar and gradually bridging toward new methods exemplifies the central message of this book: take one tiny aspect of practice, make an equally tiny change, and repeat. Keep going and keep changing. Only then will both you and your students get to experience the joy of what is truly possible in an ideal classroom space.

# I

# BEFORE INSTRUCTION

Preparing for instruction encompasses so much of a teacher's work. In fact, one might argue that the lion's share of what any instructional expert does occurs outside the classroom. The complexity of what goes into mindset, collaboration, and planning for instruction is intimidating at the outset. Just one little detail has the power to completely change the trajectory of what occurs. However, the beauty of teaching is that once everyone enters the classroom, nothing is set in stone. When teachers have effective lesson planning habits that strengthen instructional outcomes, we can embrace both successes and areas for growth with the knowledge that our most important collaborators—students themselves—are right there with us.

# Beliefs and Philosophies

*Lyla heads down the hall toward her classroom, dreading the upcoming class period. Students are supposed to be making presentations, but based on how keyed up they've been, she doubts anyone is ready. Bracing herself for a rough hour ahead, Lyla enters the room.*

*What she encounters over the next several minutes hardly comes as a surprise. Kids filter in both before and after the bell rings, making too much noise and causing disruption as they greet one another with enthusiasm. It takes Lyla almost 10 minutes to quiet everyone down, and even then, students are restless.*

*"As you know, we're doing our presentations today," she starts.*

*Before she can say another word, a girl near the front interrupts her. "What? You never told us that!"*

*Lyla can feel her face growing hot. "I absolutely did," she says, struggling to keep her voice even. "Quite a few times, actually, both verbally and in writing. This should not come as a surprise to anyone."*

*A cacophony of objections drowns out her voice as the class once more devolves into chaos. As the noise intensifies past an acceptable volume, Lyla happens to make eye contact with one of her more diligent students, a quieter boy who always does his homework. He is sitting at his desk, his materials ready, waiting to see what will happen next. His face mirrors her feelings, the frustration evident.*

I bet he wishes he were in a better class, *Lyla thinks with resentment.* I wish I were, too.

# The Insidiousness of Belief

Teachers have enormous influence in the classroom, and their perceptions of students (both individually and collectively) can make all the difference in how learning takes place. In 1965, researchers Robert Rosenthal and Lenore Jacobson conducted a study to examine the impact of labeling on student performance. They published their findings in an article entitled "Pygmalion in the Classroom" (1968), which examined the results of a social experiment. The study began with the researchers "telling teachers that certain children could be expected to be 'growth spurters,' based on the students' results on the Harvard Test of Inflected Acquisition. In point of fact, the test was nonexistent and those children [so] designated were chosen at random" (p. 16). When the study concluded, the designated students had performed better overall than their peers in the control group, demonstrating that expectation is more powerful than reality. To put it plainly, teachers developed expectations that amounted to such a strong bias that even though the entire narrative of higher achievement was false, the end results reflected the beliefs teachers held about their students.

Although the 1965 study uncovers the insidiousness of belief in a way that feels shocking, the results are hardly surprising. It is not human nature to question assumptions that have been held as truths for a long time. Over the years, for example, I have coached many teachers who are hesitant to teach advanced placement courses because they perceive that they (the teachers, not the students) are not skilled enough to handle a course that is seen as highly challenging. Each time I have encountered this hesitation, my response is that the rigor of the class refers to *student* experience. Teachers are certified in their content areas and are therefore knowledgeable. However, the perception of the attributes of a so-called "AP teacher" becomes overblown and stereotyped to the point that qualified adults balk at teaching the class. In this case, teachers don't just harbor mistaken beliefs about students; they also apply similar biases to themselves.

The premises that teachers believe to be true about themselves can be damaging, but not as much as the assumptions they may hold about students. Ideas that are mistakenly seen as innocuous can contain more harmful and perhaps even racist meanings that undermine helping kids learn and grow. Figure 1.1 shares examples of some common words or phrases that crop up frequently in conversations about kids, offers an interpretation of what they actually mean, and presents an alternative.

Many of the phrases in Figure 1.1 are ubiquitous in education. So many kids can think of times when a teacher told them that they weren't

## Figure 1.1. Insidious Phrases

| **Helpful Habit:** *Reframe your mindset to create more trusting and equitable outcomes.* | | |
|---|---|---|
| **What People Say** | **What People Mean** | **Reframing the Phrase** |
| "Not working up to full potential" | Any future progress (or lack thereof) is solely the student's responsibility. | "You are still growing in [insert specific area for focus here]." |
| "Doesn't know enough English" | Language learners are unable to make progress. (Deficit belief) | "Here are some additional words and visuals to help you read this passage." |
| "Quiet kid" | Nothing can be done to draw out or engage the student. | "How can I make this class a more comfortable experience for everyone?" |
| "Parents don't care about school." | A specific culture or economic group lacks certain values. (Biased assumption) | "What is the best way to get in touch with your family? What time of day is most convenient for them?" |
| "Behavior problem" | Misbehavior and lack of compliance are the main or only reasons why some students do poorly in class. | "What support can be provided to this student to increase engagement?" |
| "Kids can't/won't [fill in the blank]." | There is little to no likelihood that the students in question can make progress. | "Everyone can make progress with effort." |
| "Not good at" | What students can achieve is fixed and not subject to change. | "Growth is a process." |
| Referring to students as "high," "low," "quick," "slow" | Students have a fixed capacity for growth. | "This student needs scaffolding or extension with [insert specific skill here]." |

working up to "full potential." That may seem to be a well-intentioned observation, but it puts the responsibility for growth squarely with a child who is often confused and does not know what is wrong or what this end goal of "full potential" looks like. In these situations, teachers usually speak to a level of visible apathy, but more is probably happening that they cannot easily see. Either way, even students who purposely undermine their own progress deserve support. We never want to say anything that gives them the subtle impression that their teachers have given up.

Along similar lines, other phrases in Figure 1.1 ("quiet kid" or "behavior problem") represent assumptions about students that are usually not grounded in any objective data. So-called "quiet" kids are probably loud enough at home but uncomfortable in a classroom setting that for whatever reason doesn't validate their needs. A negatively labeled "behavior problem" may be trying to engage but struggles to do so appropriately. Regardless of whether adults internally or externally express damaging labels, kids are observant. They will pick up on what teachers think of them, and they will either raise or lower their performance to meet expectations.

Small but mighty changes to language can make a huge difference. For example, a knee-jerk label for children who struggle to learn might be the word *low,* but instead, thinking precisely about the obstacles each kid encounters will identify a specific area of need that removes a damaging blanket stereotype. Then, instead of saying that a child is "low," the language is more like "This student needs additional scaffolds in vocabulary comprehension to meet the grade-level standard."

Having thoughts that act as roadblocks to student success reflects habitual thinking; it is imperative to interrupt those thoughts and redirect perspectives toward a better path forward. Awareness of inner bias is a good start, but translating good intentions to specific action is the next step. It is so powerful for students to see concrete evidence that teachers believe in their capacity to learn, which can only happen when hidden barriers to productive change are removed.

# From Thought to Action: Hidden Barriers

Over time, habits form that become subversive barriers to growth for both teachers and students. For example, a teacher might think that random or "cold" calling is the best way to spot-check what kids know, when in fact the practice acts as a "gotcha" that promotes inequity as only certain kids are called on and singled out for praise or chastisement. Many teachers unwittingly hold fast to habits that perpetuate damaging outcomes, and this behavior is rooted in belief systems that have gone unchallenged for far too long.

Inner biases may control far too much of what people project externally, but people have the power to change with increased self-awareness. To receive the maximum benefits of reflection, it is important to recognize certain pervasive myths that have long been held up as norms but that are nonetheless unacceptable to continue perpetuating. Figure 1.2

## Figure 1.2. Flipping the Myth

| Helpful Habit: *Change perspective on long-held deficit-mindset beliefs.* | |
| --- | --- |
| **The Myth** | **The Flip** |
| Kids are bored and don't want to do anything. | All students have interests and want to leave their mark on the world. |
| Those who can't, teach. | Teaching is highly complex work that requires skill, insight, and intelligence. |
| Disadvantaged or "highly impacted" students don't prioritize learning. | Every student we teach wants to do well and be successful. |
| Kids won't learn unless they are entertained. | Engagement and entertainment are not the same. Engaged students will learn. |
| Teaching is a calling. You either have it or you don't. | Success in teaching is not a fixed point. Everyone can learn and grow. |
| Language learners do not have the necessary foundation for literacy. | Students who are developing fluency have knowledge to inform literacy. |
| We are fighting a losing battle with technology. | Education technology can be helpful if used appropriately and with discernment. |
| School isn't for everyone. | All students can achieve high academic outcomes if they are validated. |

provides examples of beliefs that appear regularly in discussions around teaching and learning, and it provides a "flip" to reframe harmful tenets into far more nuanced, helpful ideas.

The myths presented in Figure 1.2 are not always ill-intentioned, though some are more overtly offensive than others ("Those who can't, teach" comes to mind). Some ideas might even be seen as helpful to children. For example, someone saying that "school isn't for everyone" could wish to express that not everyone gets excited about academic subjects and that teachers should try to tap into all student interests, scholarly or not. However, that idea is too often provided as an easy out for students who are not making progress. When adults say that not everyone benefits from a formal education, they are sending a clear message to kids: *My teacher thinks I'm not smart enough to do well in school.* More often than not, these damaging messages are sent disproportionately to students of color.

Instead, translating thought to action produces far more desirable results. For example, the conviction that all students have interests of their own connects directly to targeted planning for instruction that involves all learners. Suppose a class is reading a book that is not necessarily a favorite with all students, such as John Steinbeck's *The Grapes of Wrath*. A teacher who prepares for instruction with the lens of uncovering connections that spur interest can pull from related topics that come out of the Dust Bowl period, such as climate change, extreme poverty, or societal exclusion, to get at concepts that connect more obviously to relevant student experience. Even if students cannot see themselves in the characters that course materials present, the teacher can allow them to explore alternate stories in shorter texts or media from related content that is more appealing.

To "habit stack" a mindset that is grounded in removing barriers to success, consider implementing these small steps, one by one:

1. Think about promoting equity in the classroom by exploring varied modalities for encouraging student participation (such as writing ideas on sticky notes and putting them on the walls for everyone to look at) in addition to the more traditionally requested vocal contributions.
2. Pick a strategy that best fits your current teaching style and will work most seamlessly into current instructional planning.

3. Select one day to experiment with the strategy.

4. After the lesson, reflect upon how student involvement changed or stayed constant.

5. Determine next steps, such as how to gather concrete data that will show the effect of consistent action over time.

In essence, when teachers do not accept the fundamentally flawed fallacy that students are "bored" with their learning but believe that students can engage if the circumstances allow for added involvement, the results are powerful as thoughts translate to visible differences in teaching and learning. Even better, the instructional changes that take place when flawed norms are disrupted need not be huge. Rather, it is the smaller, incremental moves to discover who students are that make the most impact.

## Counteracting Complacency

Whose job is it to ensure that broken practices are challenged and then undone? Students fall victim to systems that adults perpetuate, and it is not a child's job to fix a damaged norm. Rather, teachers must challenge their own processes and practices to achieve better results.

To that end, the self-assessment "Toolbox Timesaver" featured in Figure 1.3 provides a details-driven method for looking at areas of complacency in order to reflect and take action. The process of determining where teachers can become "unstuck" acts as a funnel of sorts. An individual might check five or six boxes in the self-assessment but then must gradually narrow the focus of growth to one single goal. Furthermore, the idea behind this tool is not to make huge, sweeping changes to practice. Rather, by selecting a small, actionable next step, the teacher who completes this process is far more likely to build successful habits.

When completing Figure 1.3, the idea is for teachers to focus thinking on small, doable changes to counteract complacency. Some actions require long-range planning for adaptive change, and attempts to accomplish them quickly are frustrating; but shorter "Band-Aid solutions" are possible for some goals and can make a significant difference

 ## Figure 1.3. Toolbox Timesaver: Am I Stuck? Self-Assessment and Action Plan

| |
|---|
| **Helpful Habit:** *Zoom in on where your practice could use the most adjustment.* |

**Directions:** Use the following checklist to determine where you might be "stuck" in your practice or perspective.

☐ *Classroom management*—Am I concerned about student behavior?

☐ *Student engagement*—Do students show interest in my class?

☐ *Collaborative planning*—Is my practice enriched by collaborating with others?

☐ *Ideas and inspiration*—Do I feel excitement and creativity when I plan instruction?

☐ *Grading and feedback*—Am I able to provide timely responses to students?

☐ *Workload*—Are my structures for managing workload effective?

☐ *Connections with colleagues*—Do I have a community of colleagues to rely upon?

☐ *Professional learning*—Am I given the opportunity to learn about what interests me?

☐ *General satisfaction*—Do I find fulfillment from being a teacher?

**Reflection**

1. Of the items you checked, pick two or three that most interfere with your putting beliefs into action. ________________________________________________

2. Think about the items you selected. Which one bothers you the most or interferes with your professional life to the highest degree? ________________________________________________________________

3. On a scale from 1 to 5 (with 5 being the highest), how much control do you feel you have over the one thing you selected as being the biggest problem? __________

**Action**

In the following table, identify what you can do immediately to take action and what might take more time. Use the example as a guide.

*Example:* Classroom management

| **Do Now** | **Wait** |
|---|---|
| • Ask for help from a colleague who has strong management skills.<br>• Create a different seating arrangement for challenging classes.<br>• Observe a class that is well-managed.<br>• Set up an incentive system for behavior. | • Look for a summer course or PD on classroom management.<br>• Gather articles/books to read.<br>• Make a plan for the first week of school next year that targets potential management minefields.<br>• Try to find a colleague who can act as a coach.<br>• Think about classroom setup. |
| **Do Now** | **Wait** |
| •<br><br>•<br><br>•<br><br>• | •<br><br>•<br><br>•<br><br>• |

as little habits are stacked on top of one another. For example, a teacher who wants to focus on workload can stack the following habits:

1. Make a list of every task that must be completed on the following day.
2. Rank the tasks in terms of priority by marking them *A, B,* and *C.* An *A* is urgent, a *B* is not critical yet but will become so, and a *C* is more of a long-term goal.
3. Look carefully at the *A* items. Think about how many of them are truly urgent, as well as which tasks might be the most dreaded and therefore difficult to manage.
4. Determine the best approach for managing the *A* workload and experiment with this approach.
5. Revisit this process again a week later to analyze what worked, what did not, and how the other categories (*B* and *C*) might be misconstrued, out of your control, or getting in the way of progress.
6. Think about how to make workload items consistently transparent and manageable, given the limitations related to personal and professional schedules.

Ultimately, although external factors can limit student progress, it is the job of teachers to determine what they can influence, control, and change for the better. By increasing awareness of some of the more accepted systems that are not serving students or even teachers' own professional growth, creating more functional methods is well within reach. Part of evolving as an educator requires a continued questioning of the beliefs and philosophies that inspired us to enter the profession, as well as making a profound commitment to ensuring that intention becomes action.

## A New Way Forward

*Lyla is excited. After the fiasco several weeks ago when students weren't ready to make their presentations, she went home and did some serious thinking. She might have been angry at first that nearly the entire class didn't seem to care about being prepared, but when she cooled off, it occurred to her that part of the issue might be stemming from the way she designs her instruction.*

*With that in mind, Lyla found one of the department veterans sitting alone at lunch the next day and decided to take advantage of the opportunity. "Can I talk to you?"*

*"Of course," Ronnie said, making space for Lyla.*

*Lyla explained what had happened in class and how frustrated she had become. Ronnie asked, "What would you change about your teaching if you could?"*

*"I've never thought about that," Lyla said, a little surprised. "But I should have. Classroom management, probably. The kids always get the better of me and disrupt everything."*

*"Anything else?"*

*"Well, I guess if I had more control of the class, I'd want the kids to be more engaged. Then they probably wouldn't act out as much."*

*Ronnie nodded. "That makes sense. So then if you had to pick something to do that gave you the most bang for your buck, what would it be?"*

*After a moment of thought, Lyla had an idea. "I gave the kids presentation topics and guidelines and never really provided any kind of choice. Would it help if I did it differently next time to give them more say?"*

*"It could," Ronnie said, "but nothing happens overnight. Figure out what kids can have more leeway with and what is nonnegotiable. And be honest about your own mistakes and wanting them to be interested in class. Maybe come up with some steps, like getting their ideas before designing your next project and then asking them for help in very specific ways."*

*Lyla promised to think about it, and she spent a lot of time crafting a different process for the presentations in the next unit. In the following weeks, although her class continued to be disruptive at times and she would need to keep figuring that part out, students had been much more excited overall to prepare for this project. Now she knows that they will be making stronger presentations because of the consistent work that groups have done together and because she has seen the drafts and steps that students created for her approval before moving forward. Lyla knows that she still has a long way to go as a teacher, but at least she's a little bit closer to where she wants to be.*

◄——————►

As conventional wisdom goes, the first step to making a change is realizing that a current state of being isn't working as well as it could. For example, Lyla has learned that building better habits gets her closer to her professional goals. Although people may be inclined to think that dramatic steps are necessary to begin the process of evolving, incremental shifts are usually far more effective and well received than seismic, more noticeable action.

Being a teacher is challenging work, and it can be tempting to give way to all-or-nothing thinking patterns that place individuals into broad categories or to make sweeping generalizations about teaching and learning in a state of frustration. To check that urge, it helps to realign beliefs in a reasonable, moderate way to ensure that good intentions equal responsive action. The brainstorming process shown in Figure 1.4 provides a quick but profound way for teachers to revisit their reason for teaching, otherwise known as their "It." By narrowing down their initial reason for entering education to one word, the focus required to identify an "It" is far more streamlined.

Narrowing down an education philosophy to one tiny detail—in this case, the "It" of our beliefs—helps us focus on what matters. In Figure 1.4, the final step of the process advises teachers to post their "It" in a place where it cannot be forgotten. The rationale for that is based on the inner workings of human nature. Although people may have excellent intentions, it can be hard to hold themselves accountable for matching an internal desire to an external response. Suppose that a teacher narrows down her one word and writes "Hope" on a sheet of paper. The meaning might not be clear to any outside observer, but this individual knows that her "It" is grounded in the optimistic vision that future generations

**Figure 1.4. Brainstorming My "It"**

---

**Helpful Habit:** *Remember the reason you got into teaching and the impact you wish to have.*

Most of us have an "It"—a reason we decided to become educators. Over time, it may become harder to identify just one thing that acts as a top priority. To focus your thinking, use the following brainstorming process:

1. Why did you get into education initially? Have your reasons for staying in the profession remained the same or evolved over time?
2. Keeping in mind your response to the first question, make a list of one-word reasons that being a teacher matters to you.
3. If you had to share just one of those words with someone else who did not know much about your work, which would you pick, and why?
4. Using a blank sheet of paper, write the one word you selected in large letters at the top. If desired, place some bullet points underneath that express the gist of your "It."
5. If desired, post your "It" in a workspace that you can easily see.

will lead the world to a better state. As such, this teacher moves through the following habits to give her actions more transparent meaning:

1. She puts her word on the wall to be more mindful of how she can express this "It" to her students through instructional methodology and to consider where she might be falling short.
2. Once a week, the teacher writes down one item that has given her hope over the last several days.
3. The teacher builds her "one item" list for several months so that it becomes a cumulative collection related to her "It."
4. Each semester, the teacher resolves to reexamine this word, change it if necessary, or continue keeping it at the forefront of her focus for another few months.

On the worst days, the actions that stem from the word *hope* can remind her that she has a larger purpose. On better days, it can inspire her to keep working toward an endeavor that she cares about deeply.

Changing a mindset can be a difficult process, especially if beliefs are deeply embedded into consciousness beyond full awareness. However, getting into the habit of challenging assumptions that have always been held up as irrevocable truths is a key step in undoing much of the damage that affects everyone in a school building when systems that enforce inequitable norms are allowed to flourish. Instead, taking small but powerful steps to dismantle a dysfunctional status-quo mindset can build habits that make way for a far more open path forward.

## Tiny Teaching Tips: Beliefs and Philosophies

"When a colleague says something that exposes a deficit mindset belief, I like to ask a question rather than confront it with a statement. If I challenge them to repeat what they said or elaborate, they rarely double down. And if they do, then I feel comfortable being more direct."

*—5th grade teacher*

"On some very good day, make a list of reasons you love teaching. Hang it behind your desk. On another day, you'll need to read it."

*—Ryan Love, high school English teacher*

# 2

# Collaboration

*"Did you see your email?"*

*Kris is clearly fired up about something, as usual. Amy, her teammate, does an inward eye roll as she turns toward her laptop. "Nope. Hold on; looking now."*

*As Amy scans the screen, Kris can't contain herself. "We're required to norm our formative assessment data each week. Like, read one another's. That is so ridiculous! Why do we have to sit in a room and do this when we can just grade our own and be done at a pace that works for us?"*

*Amy knows why Kris is angry. They've been teaching together for more than 10 years, and Kris is always the first one to be finished with her grades. She holes up in her classroom and gets it done, shunning lunch or any other distractions until the task is completed. No wonder she doesn't like the idea of group grading. For her own part, Amy doesn't feel the same way. She tends to work more slowly, and she also doubts herself more. She enjoys the collaborative nature of norming and having a colleague to bounce thoughts off of.*

*"Well," Amy says, treading carefully, "it might not be so bad. I have questions about the rubric sometimes, and it's good to have an option to ask other people what they think."*

*"Oh, please," Kris says. "Are you kidding?" As three more teachers enter the workspace, she addresses them without preamble. "Did you see the email?"*

*"Yep," one of them says. "Like I need another requirement that makes life harder. I swear, all they do in the main office is brainstorm ways to make this job impossible."*

*As the other two chime in with their assent, Amy draws into herself. She feels uncomfortable saying anything else to disagree with such clear opinions that counter her own thoughts.*

*Upset, Amy turns to her computer. Is there anything she can say or do to help the team work together without her becoming an outcast?*

## Little Missteps, Big Problems

While Amy strives to preserve the appearance of collegiality in the scenario just described, the result is that she overrides her own instincts about what is best for students out of a stronger need to appease a more vocal peer who would rather work as a lone wolf than collaborate with colleagues. In addition, Amy's fear of being excluded is significant enough that as she walks back her stance, her inner voice grows quieter until, in the end, she may come to believe that analyzing student data across a teaching team is a waste of time rather than a practice that increases the accuracy and equity of evaluation toward determining student progress.

Interpersonal dynamics in schools are notoriously tricky, and working within collaborative structures can produce results that cause people to swear off working together entirely. Educators are not by nature a group of loners; in fact, quite the contrary. Teachers enjoy gathering to talk about practice, to compare notes about students, and to engage in continuous professional learning about topics of interest. However, any negative experiences around collective work may create a lasting bias.

Furthermore, although it might seem like a small detail, the feeling of being coerced into working together can lead to complications. To put it another way, adults who might happily brainstorm ideas or problem-solve together more informally become less willing to work together when they are "voluntold" to follow processes that do not make as much sense to them—at least not at the outset. And when one considers the top-down manner in which many collaboration structures are developed, it is hardly surprising that teachers may resist participating in systems they had nothing to do with setting up.

Setting aside the complexities of hierarchical collaborative structures, inherent difficulties tend to arise whenever people work in groups. Power dynamics emerge, often based on the range on a spectrum that runs between people who dominate conversations and those who feel uncomfortable speaking up. A subtle construct identified by psychologist Irving Janis (1982) known as "groupthink" may also take over as everyone on a team strives to appear in sync with one another, when in reality their desire to not rock the boat results in undesirable outcomes as voices go unheard.

The nature of a teacher's work preference sometimes "grows out of the perceived shortcomings of the prevailing 'egg crate' model of schools. Sociologist Dan Lortie used the term to emphasize the heavily individualistic structure and culture of teaching in his classic 1975 book, *Schoolteacher*" (Schleifer et al., 2017, p. 5). The referenced "egg crate" structure refers to the compartmentalized setup of classrooms within hallways in most traditional school buildings, a physical arrangement that tends to heighten isolationism. But when teachers surmount this challenge and leave their classrooms to seek out the benefits of mutual expertise, the outcome of their work depends on how well the finer details of communication lead toward functional partnerships. So much of how collaborative structure develops is also unspoken; therefore, the benefits or drawbacks of teamwork frequently wind up being misconstrued.

To be fair, both school leaders and teachers generally do their best to create conditions that increase their chances of being effective collaborators. The motivation for doing so stems from the deep-seated belief that, together, everyone has the potential to be stronger if they are working toward a mutual goal that clearly benefits students. For example, although schools regularly set up professional learning communities (PLCs) with time set aside for collaboration, the results are variable. Little details tend to derail what might be an otherwise valid PLC process, and those insidious issues can be difficult to identify and correct. However, some patterns appear more than others. Figure 2.1 shares some of the more pervasive issues that result in PLC dysfunction.

## Figure 2.1. Derailing Details: PLCs Gone Awry

| Helpful Habit: *Keep the focus of the conversation on student growth toward a content standard.* | |
| --- | --- |
| **The Problem** | **Looks Like . . .** |
| Inequitable distribution of influence | One or two dominant voices |
| Sole focus on lesson planning | Endless loop of "What's next?" |
| Overabundance of conflict and resentment | No decisions or consensus |
| "Kid talk" consisting of idle gossip | Absence of data-driven information |
| No identified outcomes for the meeting | Conversation that is social in nature |
| Visible disengagement | One or more teachers acting passively |
| Lack of structure/organization | Aimless conversation, frustration |

As Figure 2.1 reveals, teachers who feel disenfranchised in any way by the PLC process will not benefit from working with others until, one by one, each seemingly small but significant obstacle to success is removed. To repair the damage and course-correct, Figure 2.2 shares an example of a strategy that adjusts an inequitable process, resulting in far more productive interactions.

Figure 2.2 troubleshoots the identified problem not just by giving each PLC participant a clearly delineated way to contribute to each meeting, but also by determining why the group has gathered,

## Figure 2.2. Toolbox Timesaver: Adjusting a Meeting Process

| Helpful Habit: *Make sure all team meetings include equitable ways for all voices to be heard.* | | |
| --- | --- | --- |
| **Problem:** PLC members are not given the opportunity to participate equitably in discussions that lead to decision making. | | |
| **Recommendation:** Implement a rotation to ensure that the responsibility for facilitation shifts from one meeting to the next. Each week, the facilitator shares a draft agenda, which all PLC members work on collaboratively to reach agreement about purpose and next steps. | | |
| **Purpose** | **Rotation** | **Next Steps** |
| *Example:*<br>Discuss results of the preassessment from Week 1 of the second marking period. | *Example:*<br>John—facilitator<br>Helen—notetaker<br>Maria—timekeeper<br>Nat—data collector | *Example:*<br>Identify standards of focus for the next two weeks—all members. |

identifying who is responsible for each role (facilitator, notetaker, etc.) at the meeting, and agreeing upon what follow-up is necessary. Although some PLCs assign roles for teachers that remain static for an entire year, the rationale behind regularly rotating roles is to allow for more growth, both individual and collective. In Figure 2.2, for example, Helen might be a gifted data collector with an eye toward trends and patterns. However, if Nat doesn't have an occasional opportunity to work on his own data analysis skills, he will not be able to stretch his own capacity. Furthermore, when people work in limited areas, it is not only their potential that suffers; they can also grow complacent or inattentive, which leads to a less functional dynamic for both themselves and the group.

A PLC's ultimate success is not solely dependent on fixing broken structures or repairing damaged relationships, though these are important actions to take. In addition, all participants must look beyond their own teaching lens and value how each person's distinct talents blend to form a cohesive whole.

## Collective Expertise

Defining an "expert" in any professional field can be tricky, but particularly in education, where lines tend to be blurrier in terms of who does what. Unfortunately, teachers in the United States are accustomed to having their expertise questioned by outsiders, even those who claim to have some knowledge about the education sector. In early 2023, for example, Florida school board chair Barney Bishop III responded to the firing of a principal over allowing a class to study Michelangelo's *David* sculpture by saying, "Teachers are the experts? Teachers have all the knowledge? Are you kidding me? I know lots of teachers that are very good, but to suggest they are the authorities, you're on better drugs than me" (Kois, 2023). Although it is always disheartening to see such ignorance expressed—especially by those in positions that can affect the goal of achieving student progress—it is also a disappointing cultural norm.

Dissent from laypersons is one thing. However, a far more damaging situation results when teachers begin questioning the expertise of their colleagues. Any doubts regarding the ability of others to do their jobs effectively are rooted in the seeds of distrust. Although some of the complications that cause teachers to avoid working together stem from conflicts or misunderstandings, a lack of awareness about the skills that colleagues bring to the table also interferes with more meaningful partnerships.

For teachers who seek to "habit stack" the practice of valuing everyone's expertise, the following actions can get things going in the right direction:

1. Take some time to reflect on whether you speak too much in collaborative settings or not enough.
2. If the former, practice talking less and listening more by taking a predetermined period of time (five minutes, say) just to silently and carefully consider the ideas others share.
3. If you are often overshadowed by louder colleagues, suggest a "round robin" type of structure that gives everyone a chance to share a question or an idea.
4. When responding to anyone in a group, paraphrase the thoughts expressed if you are unsure about whether you are interpreting correctly.
5. Challenge your assumptions about what others know and what values they hold, including yourself. Keep working toward more equity in team dynamics.

The ability to leverage collective intelligence is a gift, one that is too often squandered or underappreciated. When teachers come to the table already understanding the value of both individual and collective expertise, the resultant respect and trust that they feel for one another translate directly to benefits for students. Interpersonal dynamics are sometimes tricky, but they are not insurmountable. Approaching team-work with a mindset that prioritizes the strength of collaboration produces results that reap visible rewards for everyone involved.

## Avoiding the Cracks

It is not uncommon for co-teaching partnerships to be fraught with peril, nor is it unusual to see teaching teams fall apart when the division of responsibility is inequitable or dismissive of one partner's expertise. In addition, teams may experience more friction in secondary spaces. As former special education teacher Marisa Kaplan (2012) points out, "Elementary co-teachers share a classroom all day, but a middle school special education teacher can feel like a guest in a general education teacher's space" (para. 10). As a result, the misconception that one teacher in a partnership is the "main" educator in the room results in justifiable resentment from a highly qualified co-teaching partner, often in fields such as special education or English language development.

The key to avoiding an unproductive partnership lies in the specifics of how classes are planned and conducted. Though both are important, co-planning and co-teaching carry two distinct purposes. As assistant professor of education Emily Mofield (2020) explains, "Co-planning involves collaboratively developing differentiated instruction, which may or may not lead to co-teaching" (para. 6), whereas "co-teaching has been described as a way for two professional educators to 'jointly deliver instruction to a diverse group of students'" (para. 7). In theory, students derive an exponential benefit from having two skilled instructors devoted to their learning. However, when co-teachers do not establish agreed-upon norms before heading into a partnership, dysfunction or resentment nearly always follows. Figure 2.3 offers one simple framework that teaching teams can use to determine how their collaboration will move forward, from communication methods to planning responsibilities.

Although an organizer like the one in Figure 2.3 helps to establish important norms with ever-important attention to detail, any process can and should be revisited regularly as the co-teaching team evolves. Otherwise, team members will stagnate in their practice and neglect the checks and balances that ensure students are receiving the best possible instructional experience. In addition, determining who does what in a way that leaves no room for interpretation helps co-teachers know where they stand.

Digging more into the roles that each teacher occupies during instruction is also a huge determinant of ultimate success. Marilyn Friend and Lynne Cook (2009) developed six approaches to co-teaching that allow teacher teams to predetermine how they will interact with one another and with students:

## Figure 2.3.  Co-teaching Agreement: Setting Norms

| | |
|---|---|
| **Helpful Habit:** *Establish clear expectations for a functional co-teaching partnership.* | |
| **Communication** | • We will meet twice weekly. One meeting will be for planning purposes, and the other will be to analyze data and develop next steps.<br>• Timely communication will not take place after duty hours or via text; we will use our professional email accounts to share messages unless there is an emergency.<br>• In the event of absence or lateness, we will inform our partner as far in advance as possible. |
| **Planning** | • We are equally responsible for developing plans to fulfill curriculum goals and course standards.<br>• As we plan, we will embed the specific knowledge each of us brings to the table within our content area to enrich the lessons we design. |
| **Feedback** | • We will check in with each other about our co-teaching relationship each month to course-correct as needed.<br>• Students will have a quarterly opportunity to provide feedback about how our teaching-team style is suiting their learning needs. |
| **Data Analysis** | • To ensure that we both work with all students, we will divide the roster for grading and data analysis and then switch halfway through each marking period.<br>• Our data "look-fors" will reflect our teaching expertise so that all perspectives are shared equitably. |
| **Logistics** | • As we plan the week, we will also determine who is responsible for delivering elements of each instructional period based on where students can benefit the most from two instructors.<br>• We will plan for instruction using the six approaches to co-teaching, making sure to shift each approach to fit student needs. |

1. *One teach, one observe.* While one teacher takes the helm to deliver instruction, the other uses the opportunity to observe the class and develop goals for what comes next.

2. *One teach, one assist.* As one teacher leads instruction, the other assists where needed.

3. *Parallel teaching.* In this model, the class is divided into parts (usually two) and each teacher works with a smaller group of learners.

4. *Station teaching.* As students rotate through stations, both teachers move around to assist and support learning.

5. *Alternative teaching.* A larger group of students remains with one teacher as the other pulls out a smaller group to work with for a variety of reasons.
6. *Team teaching.* Simultaneously, both teachers instruct the whole class, often by taking turns as they go.

The idea behind these six approaches is not that teachers should employ the same model each day, but that they have the option to decide which avenue best fits the instruction taking place at any given time. By agreeing upon an approach together and in advance, a lot of the common disputes or resentments that crop up with inequitable distribution of work disappear. Best of all, co-teachers can sidestep the sneaky disputes that threaten to derail their success with habits that build an ideal collaborative state, one in which dream teams can flourish.

## Dream Teams

*"Thank goodness tomorrow is Friday," Amy says as she takes her customary seat at the table. "My kids have put me through the wringer this week."*

*The team had a rough start earlier in the school year, but Amy is so glad she finally spoke up and told her colleagues that she wasn't comfortable with the way they didn't prioritize looking at student data together. It turns out that a lot of people agreed with her but were afraid to say so, and Kris finally came around. She even created a team-meeting structure with rotating roles that works for everyone.*

*Today the team is clustered in Amy's empty classroom. As people open their laptops to look at a shared document, the classroom door opens and closes again as Kris enters, bearing a box of donuts.*

*"Sorry I'm late," she says, plunking the donuts on the table. "Temporary crisis, now averted."*

*Jack, who supports all emerging multilingual students, nods empathetically. "Every Friday is a crisis."*

*"Thanks, Kris. I needed this." Amy takes a donut and calls everyone's attention to the shared team-planning document. "OK, let's get down to business. This week, we were all focused on RL.3.3 to see how the kiddos were doing with character descriptions. Did everyone use 'Impossible to Train' as their text?"*

*As people nod their assent, Jack speaks up. "I will say that the kids enjoyed the topic of the story, but a lot of the vocab was complex. I had to do some scaffolding."*

*"Same," Kris agrees. "Though to be honest, I didn't just see a need for scaffolding with my special education students. I thought a large part of the class also needed support with some of the words. Like, the word* chucks *isn't familiar to most of them. We might have overreached with the text complexity."*

*Amy tilts her head, processing what she hears. "OK, but we're really talking more about RL.3.4 with word comprehension. How does the challenge with vocab relate to understanding character?"*

*"Well," another teacher breaks in, taking out a sheaf of papers, "I think it does connect. If you look at these responses to Question 3 about Jesse's pet, a lot of kids got that one wrong. I think some of the language interferes with how they interpret character."*

*"How did everyone else do on that response?" Amy asks.*

*"Similar results," Jack said, "at least in my classes. That was one of the most frequently missed questions."*

*As everyone else murmurs their assent, Amy starts typing into their shared document, describing what the group observes about student performance in relation to the identified standard. "OK," she says, pausing. "We see the issue. What should we do next?"*

*"I don't think this is about reteaching the standard necessarily," Kris says. "In my opinion, we can do a post-assessment with a different story. Let's use something with an adjusted Lexile range and see if the kids do better with figuring out who is doing what, and why."*

*"Other thoughts?" Amy asks, writing down the suggestion into their shared notes.*

*"That sounds like a good place to start," Jack says. "We need to do a better job of isolating the standard."*

*"OK, then," Amy says. "How about we look for a story that might meet the right criteria? Or should we use the rest of our team time differently?"*

*A teacher who has been relatively silent so far interjects. "We can look for stories independently," she points out. "Can we use this time to figure out what our standard focus next week will be?"*

*"I'm good with that if everyone else agrees," Amy says.*

*Sure enough, several members of the group also like that idea, and the next part of the meeting gets smoothly underway.*

Not every PLC becomes a dream team, but that doesn't mean that a desired state is unattainable. When teachers combine that awareness with structures that work, the results are noteworthy. Consider the intention behind a weekly planning tool like the one featured in Figure 2.4, which models how reflection and analysis pairs with transparency to create more effective partnerships. As the tool highlights, the featured teaching team (in this case, Ms. Johnson and Mr. Kirby) keep the learning standard as the focus of their discussion about student achievement. Rather than letting the assignment be the driver of how they determine what needs to happen next, they look for patterns from their classes to

## Figure 2.4. Shared Planning Tool

| **Helpful Habit:** *Prioritize a shared planning process that makes student thinking visible.* | | |
|---|---|---|
| **4/3–4/7** *Standard of Focus* RL.6.1: "Cite textual evidence to support analysis of what the text says explicitly as well as inferences drawn from the text." | *Assignment* Find two quotations from the text that explain the author's sadness. Then, explain how your choices connect in 1–2 sentences. | *Scaffolds* Practice identifying textual evidence; can add the analysis afterward  Graphic organizer: Connecting text to purpose |
| *Patterns* Ms. Johnson • Kids are finding textual evidence, but it doesn't connect to the analysis. • Many students are struggling with the idea of inference.  Mr. Kirby • Agreed with what Ms. Johnson observes. • Students with emerging language needs are struggling with interpreting the tone of the selected passage. | **Johnson** 4 kids: exceeding 15 kids: meeting 7 kids: not yet | **Kirby** 1 kid: exceeding 10 kids: meeting 10 kids: not yet |

*Next Steps*

1. Focus on annotating possible textual support before adding quotations to the draft.
2. Experiment with a different passage from the reading for students who may need an adjustment.
3. Have students complete a matching exercise linking quotations and purpose.

ensure that decisions reflect a larger picture of what most students, as well as select individuals, need.

With a surgical approach that prioritizes collaboration and provides a precise way to move the needle forward each week, Ms. Johnson and Mr. Kirby accomplish more than lesson planning; they also incorporate a regular examination of data into their conversation to ensure that students move forward and that instruction does not stagnate. In essence, they have created the following "habit stacks" for their planning:

1. Identify a focus standard that reflects what students need to know.
2. Determine what evidence will measure student progress.
3. Gather student data to determine their progress toward the standard.
4. Diagnose student performance and reflect upon next steps.

This sequence of steps illustrates the "backward design" approach to instructional planning (discussed further in Chapter 3).

When we think about habits that make teacher collaboration more effective, the methods that achieve a better outcome seem almost too simple: listen more, talk less, communicate with transparency and an open mind. What adult shouldn't be able to do that? However, when little misunderstandings or obstacles arise that cause tiny cracks in what already may be a shaky foundation, the entire process of teamwork crumbles. Better planning, stronger intention, and a desire to enrich the lives of students are all factors that work in tandem to help teachers do what they ultimately wish to accomplish: help students achieve their very best.

## Tiny Teaching Tips: Collaboration

"It can be hard to make team dynamics work, but I try to shut out that little voice in my head that wants to take over and do it all myself."

*—12th grade teacher*

"A good teammate isn't necessarily my best friend. It's someone who respects me but also pushes back and challenges my thinking."

*—3rd grade teacher*

# Instructional Planning

*Every Thursday, the 7th grade world studies team has a common plan-*
*ning time. Assuming no disruption from administrators or scheduling,*
*teachers meet faithfully during this 45-minute period to map out the*
*upcoming week.*

*As everyone takes their usual spots at a communal table, one of the*
*teachers has already begun to express his frustration to the group at large.*
*"Can we start by talking about how we're going to fit the second project*
*into the next two weeks? It's already March 14th. The marking period is*
*about to end."*

*The woman next to him sighs. "I was just thinking about that," she says.*
*"My kids are still working on the first one. That research project was a*
*total pain. It took forever."*

*As people begin murmuring in agreement, Denise, the team lead, feels*
*the need to provide some focus before things really get out of hand. "Wait,*
*wait. I know we're all worried and we don't have that much time. But let's*
*figure out where we are with the curriculum guide. How far behind is*
*everyone?"*

*Chris, the teacher who started this conversation, pulls up an online*
*document on his laptop and swivels it around for all to see. "The guide says*
*we should have been done with research two weeks ago, giving us a month*
*for this choice project. Is anyone on schedule?"*

*There is a silence around the table, accompanied by one or two shrugs and a few shakes of the head. Denise picks up on these nonvocal cues as a cry for help and opens up her own computer to look at the guide in more detail.*

*"Well," she says, "we can shorten the second task. It's got a learning menu, so kids could just be limited to the options that are quicker to create and grade, like the grid of Jeopardy-style clues."*

*"Do we give it the same weight as the research project?" a teacher asks.*

*Denise shrugs. "I don't think we have guidance about that, so we can probably do fewer points in the same category. That sounds fair, right?"*

*"I guess," Chris says. "But it seems so pointless to even do this project. Like, what are the kids getting out of it? I don't see the benefit."*

*"That's the curriculum for you," one of the teachers responds. "It's just a giant hamster wheel of covering one thing after another."*

*"With a regular dose of panic," another teacher adds.*

*Denise leans forward and studies the pacing guide one more time. The message is clear: this second project is nonnegotiable. She takes a deep breath and clicks into the team's joint planning document, ready to get some work done. "Let's do this," she says. "The sooner we figure this out, the faster we can just get through it."*

# When the Sky Falls: Cognitive Overload

The scenario just related is hardly unusual. In fact, one could argue that it is the norm. As dominoes collapse, it is human nature to succumb to learned helplessness. Think about what happens to one's mindset when the weight of one problem after another presents itself. An eventual meltdown or burnout is usually the result, but typically, one big event did not set the wheels in motion. Instead, just *one more tiny thing* happened, and it was enough to collapse a house of cards. Neuroscientist and psychology professor Amishi Jha (2020) creates an analogy between cognitive load and a whiteboard, which has limited space. "You can fit about three or four items on it before you max out the space. And it has one important quirk: It uses disappearing ink. Anything you 'write' on your mental whiteboard will start disappearing within a few seconds" (para. 9). The more the human brain tries to process, the greater the load becomes, which leads to higher stress.

Cognitive overload occurs when "the situation in which the demands placed on a person by mental work (the cognitive load) are greater than the person's mental abilities can cope with" (American Psychological Association, 2018). Although teaching can be a very physical job, given all the standing and moving around, the primary challenge is mental, considering how much thought must be devoted to the tiniest of details. A lesson plan that went well in first period crashes in third. Why? Students have not completed the assignment that today's class hinged upon, so now what? More than half of the class failed the district assessment, so does that mean that concepts must be retaught and remediation must occur, which in turn will throw off pacing?

Compounding matters, the daily life of a teacher is divided into a series of endless crossroads, interruptions to learning both great and small, and complex student challenges that require nuanced differentiation. It is simply too easy to become overwhelmed. It's been said that teachers make almost as many decisions in a day as air traffic controllers.

How can anyone sustain such a heavy cognitive load without experiencing eventual burnout? The answer lies in being strategic. If we think about when most teaching decisions occur, many of them are made on the fly during instructional time and cannot be predicted. However, a large number are rooted in thought processes that occur *before* students enter the classroom doors—namely, in planning time.

When teachers engage in lesson planning, the focus tends to lean on the *what* of instruction or, more specifically, the content that will be presented. Although knowing what to teach (and how to teach it) is a foundational tenet of effective practice, focusing primarily on what is essentially activity-driven instruction in the form of a series of tasks results in the feeling of planning for survival rather than for more intentional outcomes. Too often, the phrase "get through" is applied to curriculum, which is seen as something onerous to be tolerated. Teachers get stuck in a vicious cycle of spinning their wheels, planning one week after another and watching as some lessons succeed while others fail. The actual experience of communicating learning to students in a way that results in growth becomes something of a game of luck rather than a strategic endeavor. Teachers who plan for instruction in this limited way might have a series of habits that looks something like this:

1. Plan a lesson.
2. Teach the lesson.
3. Give students a quiz or test on the content within a few days.
4. Plan the next lesson.

Although nothing is inherently wrong with a cycle of planning and assessment, the subtleties of approach matter. Teachers who plan instruction from day to day and administer assessments without an overarching sense of larger purpose will always feel like they are never quite catching up. Furthermore, students who are not successful in progressing toward a clear learning goal will fall further and further behind.

Suppose there were a different pathway, one in which common planning myths were set aside and replaced with more effective processes. To begin doing things differently, Figure 3.1 presents a set of myths and corresponding "reality checks" that can help to uncover what is not working and begin the essential work of making effective changes to planning.

 **Figure 3.1. Toolbox Timesaver:
Planning Myths and Reality Checks**

| **Helpful Habit:** *Broaden the lens of planning so it stops being about survival.* | |
| --- | --- |
| **Planning Myth** | **Reality Check ✓** |
| If it's not broken, don't fix it. Lessons from prior years still work. | Repurposing lesson plans is a good place to start. However, changes from one year to the next (students, technology, etc.) should be considered before finalizing any plans. |
| If we stay one week ahead, the stress of planning is by and large alleviated. | Planning week-to-week is a survival tactic. For best results, have a clear endpoint in mind and work backward. |
| Kids can't help with lesson planning. After all, they're not instructional experts! | Although students cannot plan the content of instruction, they can provide insight into how their learning might best be achieved. |
| Collaborative planning is a waste of time. People work a lot faster alone. | Working with others might feel cumbersome, but alternative perspectives and varied skill sets lead to stronger results. |

As Figure 3.1 highlights, there is no magic bullet for lesson planning. Any meaningful change to teaching practice comes not with seismic change but with small, gradual habits that shift perspective and process. Implementing detail-oriented adjustments to practice begins with awareness, which is the purpose behind identifying myths and juxtaposing them against the reality of how to plan most effectively. To continue making progress in planning with the right priorities in mind, it is imperative to look at one of the most important (yet most frequently ignored) assets to design: student voice.

# The Nitty-Gritty: Planning for Engagement

With all the work that goes into planning instruction, seeing it go awry in execution is a painful if relatable experience. A frequent disconnect occurs between the outcomes teachers intend and actual student performance. Consider a middle school life science class that is learning about the food chain. The teacher has spent a lot of time showing students instructional videos and has provided well-constructed materials to explain concepts such as "consumer" and "food web." When students complete a quiz to demonstrate their understanding, a large percentage of them confuse the terms or cannot explain them correctly. The teacher despairs, concluding that nobody was listening to the lesson or paying attention. But is that what actually happened? Perhaps the assessment shows a lack of understanding, which points toward a flaw somewhere in the process of instruction. The question is, how can this lack of success be attributed through the proper use of data rather than intuitively?

The answer lies in how much we seek to understand the student perspective on learning. Much of the time, what seems clear to teachers is anything but to kids, for a few different reasons. First, without realizing it, teachers use a lot of "edujargon," defaulting to terms such as *benchmark* and *scaffolding* that are only meaningful to those who actively practice instruction. Second, much of what is communicated to students about their work is teacher-facing rather than student-facing; the audience of the content delivery might be students, but teachers use language that is clearer to themselves rather than to kids with phrases such as "Students have engaged in structured discourse." Instead, using kid-friendly language like "You have had meaningful conversations about the topic" is far more effective. Finally, although it might seem obvious, the established planning processes that most teachers use do not incorporate student voice. True, students might share their thoughts about their learning in unstructured ways, but how is their feedback provided before the teacher finalizes instructional plans? For the most part, this missing piece creates a chasm between a teacher's perception of how the class is working and students' points of view.

Even something as seemingly simple as framing a daily objective can become misconstrued, and students who do not understand why they are doing something remain confused. On the other hand, teachers who see framing a lesson as a series of good habits that are reinforced daily lead with transparency. Consider the teacher who engages in the following habits at the start of each class period:

1. Post an objective that explains the learning in language that kids can understand.
2. Ask students to look at the objective and paraphrase its meaning.
3. Explain how the itinerary for the day will support the objective.
4. Begin the learning with a tie-in to prior knowledge.

To effectively close the door on miscommunication of a lesson's overall purpose, it is essential to make the effort to communicate goals to students in a way that they can understand. Students might not have the necessary expertise to plan instruction (nor should they), but they can give teachers more information about how they learn. Figure 3.2 shows an example of a planning guide for student voice, which is just one way to gather a bit more information about how students see their own progress before finalizing any long-range unit plan.

The tool in Figure 3.2 may look like it requires a lot of work, but remember that this process can be implemented *selectively* as needed. Not every unit needs this kind of feedback, and teachers do not need to ask as many questions each time. It is not frequency that makes student feedback so vital; rather, the effectiveness of gathering information from classes is rooted in what happens with the qualitative data. Unfortunately, student responses tend to wind up shoved into the back of desk

**Figure 3.2. Toolbox Timesaver:
Planning Guide for Student Voice**

**Helpful Habit:** *Rather than guess what kids know, ask them directly.*

**Directions**

In our upcoming unit, we will be learning about the American Revolution. To plan the details of upcoming lessons, I need more information about your learning experiences. Please answer the following questions fully and honestly:

1. What do you know about the American Revolution? This can include anything you've heard, even small bits of information.
2. On a scale between 1 and 5 (with 5 being the highest), what is your level of interest in this unit topic? Please explain.
3. What has gotten in the way of your learning in this class in the past? To resolve this challenge, what can I do? What would you like to do?
4. What has been working for you so far in this class? What would you like me to keep doing, and why?
5. Please share any remaining information that would help me make this upcoming unit as meaningful and helpful for you as possible.

*Write your name below if you would like me to follow up with you individually.*

Name:

Thank you!

drawers rather than remain a focus for next steps, so following through on what kids share is crucial.

To get a sense of what acting on feedback might look like, see the example in Figure 3.3. The chart provides a quick method for capturing the student voice data gathered in Figure 3.2. As Figure 3.3 shows, analyzing this kind of data doesn't have to be a painful process. Analysis can be done quickly, as the teacher looks for overall patterns to serve the good of the group. The identified actions can be incorporated into adjustments in instructional planning that take into consideration what students requested.

As a final step, openly denoting how a plan changed as a result of the feedback is an essential part of closing an important loop of transparency. For example, the teacher might wish to share the voice data with students and show them exactly what has changed in the upcoming unit plan as a result. Another student-centered approach is to request help with brainstorming some of the changes. Figure 3.3 shows that students have asked for more videos, and the teacher has decided to incorporate

### Figure 3.3.  Patterns and Actions Chart

| Helpful Habit: *Take time to analyze student voice data so that students see follow-through.* | | |
| --- | --- | --- |
| **Question #** | **Patterns** | **Actions/Notes** |
| 1 | About half the students in the class referenced specific bits of information, like the Declaration of Independence or the year 1776. A few of them shared a lot more details, while the rest shared they did not have much background knowledge. | On the first day, use the factoids kids know as topic headings and have them share what they know in groups. |
| 2 | The majority of students wrote "3." A few scored their interest higher, but the second-highest group indicated a lower interest level. | With this much variation, think about more ways to apply more current topics to historical context. |
| 3 | Wow! Looks like a lot of kids don't like group work. Many of them indicated that as a barrier, along with "too much work" or "boring" class discussions. Ouch! | Consider ways to maintain collaboration with a greater variety of structures. (Talk to the team?) |
| 4 | They like the videos and resources, so that's a good sign. A lot of kids wrote "more videos," which is not particularly surprising. They also loved the social media project. | Keep what's working and think about ways to increase multimedia options without just doing more videos. |
| 5 | Didn't get much information from this question. Maybe it's not necessary to ask next time? | Make this decision at the end of the unit, and ask kids what they think before omitting this question. |
| Kids to follow up with: Gina, Jairo, John K., Lex, Manny | | |

a variety of multimedia into the upcoming learning progression on the American Revolution. Why not develop the habit of asking students to find resources as well that can be shared for the benefit of the entire class? That way, they see their own role in taking responsibility for learning.

When teachers seek to increase levels of classroom engagement by improving their habits around the overall planning process, one of the most important details may go overlooked: student voice. Gathering students' thoughts by asking the right questions and then following through on what they share before lessons are finalized sends a powerful message: their ideas count; we value and validate student thinking. When everyone in the classroom understands the power of collaborative planning, levels of interest and involvement rise to truly inspirational heights.

# The Details of Design

One of the biggest reasons teachers can get caught in a never-ending cycle of panic about what to teach next is an inherent misunderstanding of how instruction should be designed. Part of the issue stems from the natural and admirable creative skill that so many teachers possess and apply to lesson design as they create engaging activities for students. The other is rooted in the pressure of pacing, resulting in the emphasis of coverage over depth. To keep the focus on student *achievement* over *activity,* teachers must understand how the details-driven design of planning plays a vital role in ensuring that the outcomes of instruction are not just clear to all, but can also be met without unnecessary struggle or obfuscation.

◄────►

*Denise has put a lot of time and thought into how the 7th grade world studies team is functioning, and she realizes after much reflection that the PLC has been primarily focusing on the logistics of planning rather than meaningful student outcomes. With the support of her teammates, especially Chris, she has managed to design a new way to organize their meeting times.*

*Whereas every PLC meeting used to be dedicated to a conversation about what everyone has been doing and when, weekly planning meetings now have a set purpose. The team gets together every Wednesday, and the first meeting of the month is always allocated to long-range curriculum planning by backward-mapping the unit objectives. On the second week of the month, the team engages in structured "kid talk" about how students are performing on formative assessments toward the objective. And on the third Wednesday, the team has a "data chat" to look at gradebooks and determine whether students are accomplishing measurable achievement targets. Everyone has also agreed that they still need to discuss logistics and smaller details of planning, so the fourth Wednesday of the month is reserved for that, as are their informal get-togethers.*

*The process is not yet perfect, but Denise is satisfied with their progress so far. She notices a lot less of a "what are we doing" type of conversation and more focus on seeing what students still need to be able to do. In addition, some of the panic of not knowing what is happening on an almost daily basis has dissipated as the team works better together to design instruction that reaches specific goals.*

⟪————⟫

Many teachers plan instruction out of order, elevating what they think of as the "lesson plan" (but what is really simply a series of activities or tasks) over the learning target itself. In *Understanding by Design,* authors Grant Wiggins and Jay McTighe (2005) share the most frequent form of what instructional design looks like:

> Consider a typical episode of what might be called *content*-focused design instead of *results*-focused design. The teacher might base a lesson on a particular topic (e.g., racial prejudice), select a resource (e.g., *To Kill a Mockingbird*), choose specific instructional methods based on the resource and topic (e.g., Socratic Seminar to discuss the book and cooperative groups to analyze stereotypical images in film and in television), and hope thereby to cause learning (and meet a few English/language arts standards). Finally, the teacher might think up a few essay questions and quizzes for assessing student understanding of the book. (p. 15)

In this lesson design, the teacher has planned what appear to be sequential steps. First comes a tie-in between a topic or thematic focus and supportive content; next is an activity to deliver the lesson; and when instruction concludes, the teacher may (or may not) check student understanding with a high-stakes assessment.

The problem with this popular method of planning is that without what Wiggins and McTighe refer to as "explicit and transparent priorities" (p. 16), students have no idea why they are learning any particular lesson on a given day. Even more alarming, teachers may also be shooting in the dark as their vision of where instruction is headed lacks a clear endpoint. Expecting anyone to hit a blind target is unrealistic, not to mention unfair. Teachers who do not design learning with the outcome in mind wind up having no clear idea of what exactly they wish to achieve, and students are understandably even more befuddled.

The tenets of backward design that Wiggins and McTighe (2005) explain in *Understanding by Design* are laid out in three clear steps:

1. Identify desired results;
2. Determine acceptable evidence;
3. Plan learning experiences and instruction. (p. 18)

In most cases, skillful teachers who know that they must start with the first step still make one significant error: they reverse the second and third steps. Rather than determine what kind of measurable evidence will show whether students have met the desired results before they plan instruction, they first work on developing the itinerary. To help teachers feel more comfortable with changing the order in which they envision instructional planning, a template like the one featured in Figure 3.4 provides a way to organize thinking along less familiar lines. For a clear illustration of what the template in Figure 3.4 looks like with a possible lesson design, the filled-out version in Figure 3.5 imparts additional insight into how a teacher might choose to apply the components of the template to instruction.

In the filled-out version, the teacher has held herself accountable to the lesson design by bolding two important phrases: "exit ticket" and "criteria for success." This intentional reminder of backward-design thinking ensures that in the all-important planning stages, the outcome of learning remains in the foreground. Perhaps an action as seemingly

**Figure 3.4. Toolbox Timesaver: Planning Template**

| Helpful Habit: *Incorporate the nonnegotiables of backward design into planning.* | |
| --- | --- |
| **Learning Outcome** | What students will be able to do by the end of the lesson |
| **Evidence of Student Achievement** | Measurable evidence of meeting criteria for success |
| **Instructional Process** | Activities and instructional processes that will help students achieve the learning goal |
| **Lingering Questions** | Doubts, concerns, or questions that need to be addressed before instruction |

 **Figure 3.5. Toolbox Timesaver: Planning Template (Sample)**

| Learning Outcome | Students will be able to analyze two possible themes from a choice of four reading passages. |
|---|---|
| Evidence of Student Achievement | In the last 10 minutes of the class period, students will complete a short paragraph as an **exit ticket** to fulfill the following **criteria for success** that are shared with them:<br>• A clear identification of which passage you selected in the first sentence of the response<br>• A thorough explanation of the two themes you selected from the reading passage<br>• A concise and clear explanation (two to four complete sentences) of why these themes are significant |
| Instructional Process | During the class period, students will engage in activities to build their growth toward the learning goal.<br>1. Activator: Theme exploration with two film clips<br>2. Intro to Passages<br>   a. Close reading activity<br>   b. Practicing with main idea<br>3. Independent work time (reading, notes)<br>4. Summarizer and exit ticket |
| Lingering Questions | • Do students have enough background on the theme to do the activator without feeling put on the spot?<br>• How do I create extensions for students who will finish the reading more quickly?<br>• What scaffolds will students who struggle more need to complete this outcome successfully? |

small as bolding a word or two seems insignificant, but it is that teacher's infinitesimal note to self that reinforces the all-important structure of backward design.

With all the time and energy teachers put into preparing for instruction, the results should be as rewarding as possible for everyone in the classroom. Nothing is more frustrating than seeing well-intentioned plans go awry, but this experience is part of instructional practice and can be alleviated to some degree by paying attention not to every single detail but to the *right* ones. Even the tiniest move during the planning phase can alleviate unnecessary complications later on. Think of the following "habit stack" to help remember the importance of including students in lesson design so that it is possible to course-correct before things go too far in the wrong direction:

1. Write an open-ended question that asks students about their learning experiences.
2. Share the question in a way that will get a wide range of responses.
3. Think about how to incorporate student ideas into instruction.
4. Change what is possible and explain resulting actions to students so they clearly see the connection between their feedback and adjustments to instruction.
5. Ask for student suggestions throughout the process.

Part of the joy of teaching is its unpredictability. Who knows when students might do something that inspires us, that makes us laugh, or that completely exceeds our wildest expectations? Flip the coin, however, and it is easy to gradually be worn down by all the decisions, by the factors beyond our control both great and small, or by the dissonance between expectation and reality. Thankfully, the gradual process of learning to be proactive with small but mighty planning moves that make a huge difference is within reach—and well worth the effort.

**Tiny Teaching Tips: Instructional Planning**

"Ask yourself: if you were a student, is this an interesting lesson? Are the questions I'm planning thought-provoking and giving all students an opportunity to think at high levels? Do I have an activity planned so students can practice and apply the new skills they are learning? Is the activity accessible to all learners? If not, what scaffolds or supports are needed?"

*—John Jeffries, retired teacher*

"Students need to know that what they are being taught will actually matter by seeing the connection between what they are learning and how they live their lives."

*—Charles Alexander, instructional specialist*

# II

# DURING INSTRUCTION

During instruction, the magic happens when all the pieces teachers so carefully prepared come together in harmony to produce excitement and growth. The complexity of teaching and learning dictates some bumps along the road, which we can embrace as a natural by-product of productive struggle. As time goes on, what makes classroom management, student engagement, and assessing for progress smoother is building strong habits that support a laserlike focus on doing less to achieve more.

# Management

*Andre knows that he's hit the jackpot with his mentor teacher. Ginny is a formidable classroom expert, someone who makes the job look easy.*

*But as Andre also knows too well, he doesn't get the same results when Ginny leaves for a few minutes and lets him take over the class. When she's in charge, kids move smoothly through the class period, focus on tasks without complaint, and make visible progress. When he takes the helm, they test the waters in ways that are incredibly frustrating.*

*Take yesterday, for example. Andre planned a fun warm-up to teach figurative language to his class. The idea was for kids to act out examples and to enjoy being a little silly. Unfortunately, some students took the exercise way too far, and one particularly lively kid named Freddy actually tried to leave the classroom via the first-story window to demonstrate the difference between literal and figurative meaning.*

*And yet, when Ginny teaches an engaging lesson, kids never try to push her boundaries. Andre knows that he lacks experience and the cachet of being the "real" teacher in the minds of the 5th graders he works with, but he wishes he could do better.*

*Now, he sits with Ginny during their planning period. He's quieter than usual, and she notices. "Is something wrong?"*

*"Sorry," Andre says, running his hands through his hair. "It's just that this whole student teaching experience is harder than I thought it would be."*

*"Is this about yesterday?"* Ginny had walked in just as Freddy was trying to climb out the window, and she had helped defuse the situation without showing the slightest hint of annoyance at anyone; but Andre is still embarrassed. *What teacher can't stop a 5th grader from behaving that way?*

*"A little. I mean, yesterday didn't help. But the kids keep trying things with me that they would never dream of doing with you, and it's starting to get to me. What if my own classes do that next year?"*

*"Every new teacher I've ever mentored worries about this,"* Ginny says, *"and it's a legitimate concern. Classroom management is hard, even with your own classes. It gets better with experience and with a solid plan going into the year for structures and routines. But can I make another suggestion?"*

*"Of course. Please."*

*"So, the warm-up you did yesterday?"* Ginny pauses, and Andre nods to urge her to continue. *"It wasn't challenging enough. The class has learned about the basics of figurative language already, so what you did is old hat. When kids aren't presented with something that stretches their thinking, they are far more likely to act out."*

Andre frowns, thinking about this. *"But it was just a warm-up."*

*"Right,"* Ginny confirms, *"it was. And what is the purpose of a warm-up, do you think?"*

*"Well, I guess it's to get them ready for learning."*

*"Ready how?"*

*"Ready, like in their seats, in the right frame of mind."* Andre looks at Ginny. *"Isn't that what a warm-up is for?"*

*"Arguably, sure,"* Ginny says. *"What you're describing is something that is designed for behavior, not for learning. They already know what the warm-up is focused on, and you're just trying to set the stage. My question is, for what?"*

Andre shakes his head. *"I don't understand."*

*"What happened after the warm-up? Did kids learn something new related to the exercise, like how to write a specific product using figurative language? Was it related to a curriculum objective?"*

*"Oh,"* Andre says, thinking about it. *"No, not really. It was just supposed to be fun."*

*"And was it?"*

*"Well, not for me,"* Andre admits. *"And maybe not for anyone else either. Not even Freddy. He seemed kind of surprised at himself."*

*"I agree. But do you know why it wasn't fun?"*

*"I'm starting to think I do, but you tell me."*

*"Because,"* Ginny explains, *"warm-ups tend to exist in a bubble. They don't prepare kids for new learning by tapping into prior knowledge to extend it further to a more challenging concept. Instead, they don't make much sense to anyone. And sometimes there's a place for that. But usually it's better to use an activator to start your lesson."*

*"An activator? Isn't that the same thing?"*

*"The warm-up and activator are both used at the start of the lesson, but they have one key difference. Activators do what they describe: they activate what kids know. They also connect to whatever comes next in the class period. Warm-ups don't do that."*

Andre nods. *"OK, I get that. But what does that have to do with everyone going crazy yesterday?"*

*"You didn't challenge them,"* Ginny says. *"Instead, you lowered the standard of their learning with an exercise that had nothing to do with what they were doing the day before or what would come next. They didn't see the point. And when kids don't see the point, they respond erratically."*

*"But isn't that really a discipline problem?"*

Ginny shrugs. *"That is probably the most apparent thing to look at. But to me, almost all classroom management issues, disciplinary or otherwise, start with instruction. When your teaching is fundamentally flawed, kids don't behave the way we want them to. Instead of looking at it from the limited perspective of behavior, widen your scope. Think about what you're teaching them. When that is in order, everything else tends to fall into place."*

Andre sits back to digest Ginny's thoughts. *"I never thought of it that way before."*

*"That's why you have me,"* Ginny says with a smile. *"And we have some planning to do. Want to show me what you're thinking about for the project coming up?"*

*"Sure,"* Andre says, opening his laptop. *"I've got some ideas."*

As he starts to take Ginny through his work, she watches as he adjusts some of the approaches he had initially planned that might not work for this age group. He'll figure it out, *she thinks.*

# Discipline or Management?

Though he has likely spent a lot of time observing Ginny in action, it takes a heartfelt conversation with his mentor for Andre to understand that when he teaches content that is not appropriate for his students, they respond by testing the limits of his tolerance for their behavior. Like so many inexperienced teachers before him, he assumes that discipline, in isolation, is the issue he faces, mainly because he is new at this job and the class does not technically "belong" to him. However, as Ginny reveals, deeper reasons explain why students react so differently to her.

When new teachers are asked to share what makes them most anxious about starting the school year, they overwhelmingly point to classroom management as a significant stressor. In a 2014 study conducted by the National Council on Teacher Quality (Greenberg et al.), researchers found that "for new teachers, the strain of trying to deliver sufficiently engaging instruction and at the same time orchestrate appropriate behavior can be intense, overwhelming and ultimately defeating" (p. i). Considering that veteran teachers can experience the same struggle many years into their careers, everyone stands to benefit from having a repertoire of classroom management strategies that fit a variety of learners.

The terms *discipline* and *management* are often used synonymously, especially by less seasoned educators or people outside the profession. Discipline is one aspect of a well-managed classroom, but it is not anywhere near the full picture of what needs to happen for learning to run smoothly. It might not be immediately reassuring to tell an inexperienced teacher that classroom management encompasses so much more than discipline, but upon reflection, it helps to understand the minute aspects of what goes into a functional space for teaching and learning.

One way to start piecing out where discipline and management diverge and where they come together is to complete a chart like the one in Figure 4.1, which allows either individual teachers or teams to look at scenarios, think about where they fall, and discuss how to categorize each example.

Typically, an issue is designated as disciplinary if a consequence (logical or otherwise) is attached to student behavior. As with so many

### Figure 4.1.  Discipline or Management?

| Helpful Habit: *Distinguish classroom management from disciplinary action.* | | | |
|---|---|---|---|
| **Scenario** | **Discipline** | **Management** | **Both** |
| Each day, the teacher greets students at the door by name. | | | |
| A student is given an alternative assignment because she says the original is "boring." | | | |
| On the first day of school, students receive assigned seats. | | | |
| When students are distracted, the teacher stands nearby to focus their attention. | | | |
| The teacher uses a variety of community builders to establish relationships. | | | |
| A student is given detention for refusing to comply with a teacher directive. | | | |
| When the teacher raises one hand, students do the same and grow quiet. | | | |
| Students establish classroom behavior norms in collaboration with the teacher. | | | |

complex topics, however, a few of the scenarios in Figure 4.1 overlap somewhat. For example, when a student resists completing assigned work, that lack of compliance could be managed or disciplined. With the former, the teacher finds a way to engage the student and get her to do something. However, some teachers apply disciplinary measures by sending kids out of the classroom, calling home, or withholding some type of privilege until the work is done.

Although discipline has its place, it is not usually the most effective way to mitigate an existing or potential conflict. When teachers have consistent classroom structures and routines in place, students are less likely to become distracted and act in undesirable ways. Just as important, the strength of instruction plays a significant role in how focused kids remain on the work at hand. If lessons are not engaging, are not geared toward the appropriate grade level, or fail to support students' sense of identity, students are more prone to misbehavior.

It therefore becomes highly important to know which tiny details of classroom management to focus on by getting to the root of what works and what gets in the way of creating a learning environment that supports student achievement. Making learning clear to kids sets the right tone and can be accomplished through "habit stacks" that establish an environment that is set up for growth. Here is an example:

1. Ensure that the lesson has an accessible entry point while learning standards remain high.
2. Have students engage in an activator that clearly connects to the daily objective.
3. Ensure that students see the link between the activator and new content by framing the lesson with explicit tie-ins and by using kid-friendly language to explain learning targets.

Like so many aspects of teaching, small management habits build upon one another to make a huge impact over time as long as we show students what to look for and why it matters. When students do not understand the purpose of their learning, they are more likely to act out. Conversely, when they see the importance of each day's planning, their awareness leads to far more productive engagement.

## The Root of Management

When an observer enters a chaotic classroom space, it is easy to assume that the teacher in charge is simply unable to control student behavior. After all, as doctors are often taught in medical school, "When you hear hoofbeats, think horses, not zebras." This approach to diagnosis (also sometimes known as Occam's Razor, named after William of Ockham, a 14th century English theologian and philosopher) dictates that the simplest or most obvious cause of a problem is usually the correct one. Applied to classroom management, a teacher who struggles to control a room full of rowdy students clearly has a problem with discipline. Therefore, the heart of the issue must be rooted in behavior management strategies that are either ineffective or absent, right?

Well, maybe. It could be that the biggest problem is confined solely to the way behavior is managed, and that given the right strategies and consistent application, students will become compliant. In a situation like that, any issues can be identified and solved with the guidance of experienced mentors or coaches. However, when classes have gone off the rails to the point that a learning space reflects a larger instability, the temptation to oversimplify and confine the teacher's needed growth solely to mitigating student behavior is flawed to the point of misdiagnosis.

In reality, classroom management is divided into many areas. As education consultants Jon Saphier and his colleagues (2018) explain, "Competent handling of Attention, Momentum, Space, Time and Routines forms a foundation for good student behavior" (p. 123). The first item on this list, attention, is a continuous worry for teachers. *How will I get my students to stop talking and listen to me? Once they are calm, how do I keep them from becoming distracted? And what do I do if they can't focus on the task at hand?* These are valid concerns for all teachers, not just newer ones, and they tend to present themselves as challenges with each new group of students.

It is therefore vital to understand why classroom management can become challenging and to develop a plan that is designed to proactively create the most functional learning spaces possible. For example, Saphier and his colleagues (2018) list a bevy of reasons that teachers fail to maintain order in their classrooms, including "inappropriately matched or boring work," "student sense of powerlessness," "confusing instruction," and "student not knowing how to do the expected behaviors" (p. 123). When kids act out, identifying exactly why that happens is crucial to making effective change.

As Ginny points out to Andre in the earlier scenario, the most common cause of student distraction is rooted in a lack of instructional clarity. How can teachers make sure they incorporate the right details into each class period to support a well-managed environment in a way that is clear to students? The answer lies in specific actions, known in schools as "look-fors," that ideally recur every single day. When teachers build the habit of ensuring that the correct structural pieces are in place to support student learning, management goes much more smoothly. Even more important, there is a strong link between the elements of good initial instruction and a classroom that is more likely to produce equitable outcomes. The following list consists of habits that teachers should use each day in the classroom:

- Communicate the learning objective in student-friendly language.
- Explain the learning for the day.
- Provide an itinerary for the class.
- Continuously check for student understanding.
- Work to mitigate confusion.
- Differentiate activities and assignments as needed through scaffolding or extension.
- Create equitable opportunities for students to ask questions, engage in conversation, and share their voices.
- Provide appropriate materials and resources to help explain the learning.
- Communicate the criteria for success on tasks in student-facing language and provide transparent feedback that is objective and free of implicit bias.
- Use assessment (both informal and formal) strategically to uncover what students know and what they need to work on.
- Provide students with varied opportunities to demonstrate their knowledge.

On the face of it, this list might seem like way too much to handle in one class period. However, many of the pieces are brief, detail-driven actions that make a huge difference in student learning. In addition, many of the look-for items in the list in Figure 4.2 are geared toward transparency, or what is sometimes called a "no-secrets" classroom. For example, teachers who frame the day's learning in student-friendly terms have their audience firmly in mind every time they plan instruction. Along similar lines, students who are assessed each day (usually informally, but also with more official methods) have teachers who are fully informed about where learning needs lie. From a management perspective, so many pieces fall into place when teachers are more confident about presenting a lesson that has been carefully prepared with an end goal in mind. Just as important, the consistency that results from building the habits listed in Figure 4.2 makes way for stronger classroom structures.

**Figure 4.2.  Class Structure**

Helpful Habit: *To create added clarity and transparency, be sure that every class has a clear structure.*

1. Engage students in an activator.
   a. How can prior knowledge be activated to help students approach new concepts that are arising today?
   b. What will make this activator engaging?
   c. Are students sometimes given opportunities to help design the activator?
2. Share the daily learning objective.
   a. Does the objective clearly identify age-appropriate content standards that students will achieve by the end of the learning today?
   b. Is the objective measurable?
3. Frame the learning. Why are we here?
   a. Is the framing phrased in student-friendly terms and with an inclusive lens?
   b. Has the teacher explained why the objective is important?
4. Go over the daily itinerary.
   a. What is happening today, and who is responsible for each piece of the lesson?
   b. Do students share responsibility for their learning?
5. Begin the learning activity for the day.
   a. How should this lesson be structured? Is it teacher-directed, student-centered, or a combination?
   b. Will students remain in one place or move during the period?
   c. What options for differentiation have been provided?
6. Ask students to summarize their learning; collect formative data.
   a. How will student learning be measured at the close of the period?
   b. What can students share that will help the teacher determine next steps?

# The Role of Structure

In a thoughtfully structured learning environment, a class almost seems to run itself, but it is not the effortless endeavor that it appears to be. So much goes into creating such a space, and teachers have all sorts of ways to get there. That said, certain elements tend to appear across classes that are taught skillfully. Figure 4.2 offers a traditional class structure sequenced by the classic parts of a sound instructional period, as well as some important considerations for each.

Details matter, and figuring out how to answer each question in Figure 4.2 builds teaching habits that become second nature. Naysayers might argue that even with all the elements of structure in place, a class can still devolve into chaos. That is always a possibility, but one thing is certain: without structure, management challenges are almost guaranteed and will become increasingly severe, distracting from student learning and achievement. When teachers habitually apply a structure like the one exemplified in Figure 4.2, they not only have more time and space to handle their classes with a bare minimum of control, but can also put more energy into matching the small but powerful tools in their repertoire to the students who sit in front of them.

## Making a Match

*Ginny sits next to Andre, who is busily cutting larger pieces of paper into little squares. "What are you working on? You're not even eating your lunch."*

*Without looking up, Andre says, "Yeah, I know. I just had this idea for our last class today, and I want to give it a shot."*

*"You're making flash cards?"*

*"Not exactly. I was thinking about how we talked about figurative language, and I realized that the kids know a lot of the basics. But I think they have a hard time recognizing more complex techniques in a random context without more support, so I've created a way to challenge them more."*

*"Is it a game?" Ginny asks.*

*"Pretty much," Andre says. "This is something I made up in my head today. They're going to do an interactive matching exercise that is a whole lot more rigorous than the warm-up that tanked the other day."*

*Ginny leans forward to look at a card. "Helen knows that if she fails her test today, she will literally die," she reads aloud. Looking up at Andre, she guesses. "Hyperbole? Not to mention a total misuse of the word literally?"*

*"Right," Andre says. "For that one and a few others, they have to focus on the best way to describe the scenario they pull. I figured that will help them prepare for all the multiple-choice items that always ask for the 'best' answer and that seem so confusing."*

*Ginny examines more cards. "Hmm. A lot of these are similar. Types of metaphors, for example."*

*"I put tiny differentiations in the cards that separate one figurative technique from another. That's what makes this exercise so challenging, but I hope in a good way. We've learned all about these terms on paper, but the question is whether the kids will be able to apply what they learned*

*correctly when they walk around trading cards and having conversations with one another to come to some kind of agreement."*

*"Why do they have to agree?"*

*"I thought it would be more fun that way, and I'm always trying to increase productive student discourse," Andre says. "If they're engaged, I'm hoping not to have the same issue that came up with behavior."*

*Ginny sifts through the cards. "Will our other classes play this game?"*

*"They might. It depends on how this goes. I want to see if the class I find the most difficult to manage can respond better, and then I'll think about what to do with our other classes and what they need."*

*"So, this is about management?"*

*"Partly," Andre says. "But I'm hoping that when the kids are into what we're doing, I won't have to worry as much about whether they'll behave. And even if they get a little excited, it's fine if they're still focused."*

*"Makes sense. Sorry for all the questions, but I wanted to make sure I understood," Ginny says. She gestures toward the cards. "Need help? I have scissors, and I've eaten."*

*"That would be awesome," Andre says. "My stomach just rumbled, big time."*

◄──────►

As Andre plans a slightly different pathway for his last class of the day, he knows that although all students must meet the same standard of learning, their journey in getting to a desired point can be different. As Saphier and his colleagues (2018) point out in *The Skillful Teacher,* a significant skillset in teaching involves matching the appropriate instructional strategy to students in the classroom. This "matching" occurs when teachers are "making decisions about which tool will be most effective to use in a given situation" (p. 14). Otherwise, even with the best possible strategies in our repertoire, a class period can go south when the lesson plan doesn't align with student needs. That is why a lesson plan that worked beautifully in prior years, or with other groups of kids, can suddenly tank without warning. However, when students are excited about what they learn and see their own growth, the higher levels of engagement that result are well worth the time it takes to ensure that structures and processes are effective.

One of the biggest reasons that classroom management becomes so intimidating is that very small moves can be the difference between a successful learning environment and a chaotic one. It sometimes feels scary that these small moves potentially result in huge (and sometimes unwanted) results, and it can take a long time to figure out how to put the pieces together. Gradually building good habits around how learning is structured is an incremental process, not a make-it-or-break-it single action that determines a teacher's entire future if things don't go smoothly on any given day. Even the most skillful teachers still encounter challenges around management, and it is only through experimenting with the details that we can finally discover what works best for students.

**Tiny Teaching Tips: Management**

"Without an authentic purpose for the work, students lack motivation or resolve, so they don't attempt the assignment or task. This disengagement manifests in behavior issues. Have an authentic purpose!"

*—Elizabeth Jorgensen, high school English teacher*

"Classroom management sounds so scary, but it's really about having a plan, understanding that some days are better than others, working to make changes that improve learning, and not giving up."

*—Kindergarten teacher*

"When partnering students for conversation, use a community builder such as, 'The person who woke up the earliest shares first.' This provides a brief getting-to-know-you activity and also structures the conversation so one person doesn't always dominate the conversation."

*—John Jeffries, retired teacher*

# 5

# Engagement

"*Can you believe it?*" *Mr. Jasper asks.* "*There are 206 bones in the human body. Is that surprising?*"

Nope, *Kylie thinks to herself. I've seen* Grey's Anatomy.

*For the next hour, Mr. Jasper goes over some of the more significant bones in the body as students fill in a worksheet that has blank spaces for each bone. Kylie obediently copies down each one: tibia, femur, sacrum. Her pen moves independently of her brain, which isn't really processing much of what she's writing.*

"*We're going to have a quiz on this tomorrow,*" *Mr. Jasper announces to the sound of several groans.* "*I know, I know. But all will be well.*"

*That night, Kylie pulls out her worksheet and looks it over. As she's frowning over the vertebrae (how many kinds are there?), her mom walks by and looks over her shoulder.*

"*Oooh, fun,*" *her mom says.* "*I remember learning about this. Isn't it cool?*"

"*Not really,*" *Kylie says with a shrug.* "*I don't like thinking about what's under our skin. It's gross.*"

*The next day, Kylie takes the quiz. Her memory doesn't help her as much as she hoped it would, and on top of that, there are questions that she didn't anticipate about how the bones function. She leaves feeling a little down. That feeling only gets worse the next day, when Mr. Jasper asks*

*Kylie if he can talk to her. When she goes to his desk, the quiz is sitting right there with a letter C on top.*

*"I wanted to talk to you about this, Kylie. You seemed to be attentive during the lesson, but then your quiz grade doesn't really match up with that. Can you tell me what might have happened?"*

*"It's not a bad grade," Kylie says, feeling defensive.*

*"It's not the grade I'm concerned about, though I do believe you can do better," Mr. Jasper says. "I'm more curious about what threw you off."*

*"The questions about how bones work," Kylie responds. "Like this one. How was I supposed to know that we use our cervical vertebrae to nod our heads?"*

*Mr. Jasper frowns. "I told you that yesterday," he says. "It was one of my examples. Perhaps you didn't hear me?"*

*"But I thought filling out the sheet was the important part."*

*"The important part is what we call 'application.' Do you know what that means?"*

*Kylie shakes her head, and Mr. Jasper points at her motion. "See? Cervical vertebrae." He chuckles, but she just looks at him. "Sorry. It means that science class isn't just about memorizing facts. It's about figuring out how they work in a larger sense, why they matter."*

*"But in 6th grade, we just needed to memorize the words. We even had open-note quizzes."*

*"I can't speak to that experience," Mr. Jasper says, "but in 7th grade and from now on, you'll need to have a deep level of knowledge about what we learn. So, let's practice."*

*"Now?" Kylie asks, startled.*

*"No time like the present," Mr. Jasper says, pulling out his smaller model skeleton. "Do you play any sports?"*

*"Softball," Kylie says.*

*"OK, then tell me. What is a bone you would need to use when you pull your arm back to throw the ball?"*

*Kylie examines the skeleton. "It's pretty obvious, right? Like, anything in your arm. The radius? Carpals?"*

*"To a degree. But think about it. Actually pull your arm back, like you're going to throw the ball. Come on," Mr. Jasper urges, as Kylie glances self-consciously at her classmates who are working in groups. "You can do it."*

*She complies, and he nods at her in encouragement. "OK, that's good. But do it more slowly, and stop when your arm pulls all the way back."*

*With Kylie's arm behind her, Mr. Jasper smiles to keep her at ease. "Great. What part of your skeleton is working right now?"*

*She thinks about it, concentrating. Suddenly, her brow clears. "It's my back, isn't it?"*

*"You tell me. What part?" Mr. Jasper holds a copy of the skeleton worksheet in front of her.*

*"My scapula?"*

*"Bingo!" Mr. Jasper says. "That bone back there? We call it the shoulder blade. When you pull your arm back, it moves toward the middle of your back. There should be a nice range of movement there."*

*"There is," Kylie agrees, moving her arm back and forth.*

*"And when athletes get injured, doctors and physical therapists use what they know about bone structure to help people recover."*

*"Muscles too, right?"*

*"Sure. That's another piece of the puzzle."*

*At that, Kylie nods and looks at the skeleton, then back at Mr. Jasper. "This makes a lot more sense now. And I can see why it's interesting to be a physical therapist. My aunt does that. I should talk to her."*

*"For what it's worth, I probably could have given everyone more time before taking the quiz. I'm offering a retake on Friday. Interested?"*

*"Absolutely."*

*"Great. Then use the time to study and let me know what questions you have. Remember, what are you focusing on?"*

*"I don't remember the word you used," Kylie says, "but I think it's about making sure I understand how the bones work, not just where they are. Like, really getting what they do."*

*"Application, and yes. Exactly."*

*"Thanks," Kylie says, and heads back to her seat to grab her things for the group work everyone is doing. She feels a whole lot better now.*

## What Is Engagement?

Reaching out to students who are sitting in an unobtrusive middle ground might seem like a low priority when other kids in the class are struggling more noticeably. Kids like Kylie, for example, do just well enough that teachers often fail to notice their level of disengagement. They may strive to be invisible, doing their work and exhibiting behavioral compliance that allows them to fly under the radar. Unless students like this have a teacher like Mr. Jasper, they may never reach a deeper level of cognitive engagement in their coursework unless it occurs accidentally.

As teachers know all too well, engagement is a concept that is difficult to define. Often mistaken for entertainment, the idea of students enthusiastically responding to class content can become a futile pursuit in classes that do not seem to be reaching their target audience.

Classroom structures that rely on external motivation to push students into action have results that are relatively superficial. As I write in the student-centered guide *Teach More, Hover Less: How to Stop Micromanaging Your Secondary Classroom* (Plotinsky, 2022), "When we rely on externally motivating factors to engage students, such as grades, any buy-in we get is a result of students' surface-level desire to achieve in a particular teacher's class" (p. 42). Take traditional grading systems as an example of this "surface level" of engagement. True, some students may show a more profound interest in course content that goes beyond a letter grade, but that is not the norm. Rather, the extrinsic motivator of a metric that goes on a school transcript can inspire many kids to approach their learning with a certain degree of added attention. Unfortunately, keeping engagement in an external realm leads to two specific problems. First, many students need internal drive as a push to achieve in the longer term. Second, motivation that comes from the outside is transient; a deeper connection to content isn't possible without a more genuine desire to learn something for its own sake.

Thinking about what it means for students to demonstrate engagement, we see that some of the most visible signs of involvement are also the most deceptive. Figure 5.1 provides examples of behavior that is often misconstrued as meaningful interest and gives counterexamples that indicate a far more profound investment in class.

The more obvious indicators of engagement are not nearly as authentic as smaller, subtler signs. Consider how strongly visible behavior can mislead the impressions we form. If students are awake and alert,

**Figure 5.1. Signs of Engagement**

| Helpful Habit: *Look beyond what students visually exhibit to determine how engaged they are with class content.* | |
| --- | --- |
| **Superficial Engagement** | **Deeper Engagement** |
| Visual cues (nodding, eye contact, smiling) | Evidence of higher-order thinking through questioning |
| Repetition of information | Elaboration of ideas beyond what is taught in class |
| Rote memorization of content | Expressed interest in taking the learning beyond what is presented |
| Appearance of attention (note taking, sitting up, level of alertness, physical presence) | Genuine desire to understand concepts for the sake of learning itself |
| Doing only what is required | Taking on shared responsibility for the learning process |

answer questions that teachers pose, and comply with what is asked of them, they are generally seen as being highly engaged in the class. However, as Figure 5.1 highlights, what is apparent to the eye can also be inaccurate. Someone who presents the appearance of involvement may be internally disconnected from whatever is happening, or perhaps just doing the minimum that is needed to hit a certain threshold for success.

When students are truly engaged, their behavior reflects genuine interest in learning, which can be harder to spot. They might pose insightful questions or express a desire to move beyond what is immediately being presented to reach another layer of knowledge. For teachers, learning how to differentiate superficial engagement from something more significant depends on being able to pinpoint what a desired state looks like. If we habitually recognize the details of what we're looking for, it becomes that much easier to find the holy grail of student engagement.

# Three Types of Engagement

Sometimes the biggest barrier to school success is a breakdown in communication on a seemingly minute level: jargon. Educators use the same terms, but they can mean very different things in people's minds. For example, the phrase *academic language* could refer to the way students are expected to speak in classroom settings. Or, academic language might be a reference to Tier II vocabulary words, which reflect a higher level of complex application. Similarly, the term *engagement* comes with any number of associations, and the dissonance that results in how people might interpret this concept results in a surprising number of complications. For example, if one teacher sees student engagement as participation in class whereas another sees the quality of classwork as a sign of genuine involvement, kids receive all kinds of mixed messages about what is expected of them. Multiply that confusion by all the teachers students will work with over the course of many years, and the problem becomes significant.

If we want to ensure that everyone defines engagement in like terms, it is essential to be clear about its meaning. To that end, education researchers Jennifer A. Fredricks and her colleagues (2004) identified three types of student engagement:

> Behavioral engagement draws on the idea of participation; it includes involvement in academic and social or extracurricular activities and is considered crucial for achieving positive academic outcomes and preventing dropping out. Emotional engagement encompasses positive and negative reactions to teachers, classmates, academics, and school and is presumed to create ties to an institution and influence willingness to do the work. Finally, cognitive engagement draws on the idea of investment; it incorporates thoughtfulness and willingness to exert the effort necessary to comprehend complex ideas and master difficult skills. (p. 60)

When we examine these three types of engagement, we can see a progression of sorts that occurs in the sense that it is better for students to reach cognitive engagement than to remain mired in the behavioral realm. However, because of the traditional rewards systems that currently dominate educational institutions in the United States, many people reach adulthood without ever moving past compliance and cooperation to achieve the feeling of having true interest in their work.

To move the needle in fractional, doable increments for students so that their engagement isn't based on transient factors such as external motivation or an emotional connection that could grow tenuous or disappear, once again it becomes crucial to zoom in on tinier yet significant habits such as these:

1. Make a conscious effort to talk less.
2. Observe a class and tally student responses. Who is talking, and how much?
3. Gather other relevant data for more equity-related purposes, such as information related to who is most involved in a class.
4. Assess which type of engagement each of your students most often demonstrates.
5. Analyze results to determine where inequity lies with student involvement.
6. Adjust instruction to reach students who are exhibiting only more surface-level engagement.

Ultimately, having a room full of students who are excited about what they learn doesn't happen in one fell swoop. Instead, teachers who use purposeful practices to pay close attention to how students respond to instruction are more likely to reach each individual in meaningful ways.

## Reaching Out

It is likely that when a classroom observer sees students exhibit a strong sense of shared responsibility for the work they do, the teacher has consciously built that environment piece by piece. Nurturing strategies that allow for more profound interest is best done in small doses. As one habit becomes regular practice, teachers can gradually stack more actions on top of one another so that all students are more likely to experience cognitive engagement.

To get a sense of what types of engagement habits can be stacked, the following list shares a bank of options that put students at the center of their own learning. To try out some of the items on the list appropriately, I recommend starting with just one habit that speaks the most to existing practice. Improving student engagement doesn't require reinventing the wheel. Rather, the largest impact will come from a more targeted, one-by-one application of these strategies:

- *One Question.* At the close of instruction, collect a single question from each student about the day's learning. This practice helps to uncover confusion, give students more voice, and provide a safe avenue for expressing concerns.
- *Revolving Door.* On one day each week, a small group of students is responsible for developing a learning activator in collaboration with the teacher. Although this interaction can occur offline, a short planning session during class while the rest of the students work independently is ideal to give the teacher a chance to determine how well the activator connects to content.
- *Choice of Three.* Select three agenda items that need to occur within the span of a few days' time. Rather than dictate what students do at specific times, allow them to self-select what they work on in any given class period.
- *What Do You Think?* Ask students to write down on a small strip of paper one statement that expresses what is working about their learning, and what could make it better.
- *Gamify It!* Rather than review content in a traditional way, let groups of students create games that teach core concepts in an accessible way.
- *It's a Draw.* For visually oriented students, provide an opportunity to create or draw an image that reflects a core learning concept.
- *Choose Your Own Adventure!* Rather than dictate a specific format for an assignment, share the learning goal and criteria for success with students and give them various options for how they will fulfill identified outcomes (or let them decide for themselves).
- *What I Know.* Give students an opportunity to share what they know about a topic on a sheet of paper. Then, put them in groups to teach one another about what they wrote. Finally, gather all the papers and create a handout to share with the class as a resource.

Teachers who prioritize engagement also keep equity at the forefront of their focus. To reach all students, instruction needs to be many things: grade-level appropriate, aligned to content standards, and engaging. With these priorities in mind, students must also be given access and opportunity to grow. When they struggle, it is the teacher's job to scaffold them upward toward the standard of learning and keep expectations high, not lower the bar. When students exhibit a need for enrichment, providing extensions is also an incredibly important aspect of differentiating instruction while holding everyone in the room to the same standard. Then, with strategies for engagement like the ones in the preceding list, all students can access course content.

When teachers take the time to apply their focus to all students and not just the ones who cry out for attention, the overall engagement level of a class rises. Classrooms are finely wired places. Just one small ripple of change can rock the instructional boat—in a good way. Setting productive adjustments in motion is easier when everyone in a school has a common understanding of what it means to be engaged; when we pay attention to subtle signs of disengagement; and when tiny habits, slowly stacked on top of one another, allow students to feel much more invested in their learning.

## Tiny Teaching Tips: Engagement

"Keep equity at the forefront by ensuring all students can access the grade-level assignments and recognizing all students bring knowledge."

*—Elizabeth Gamino, instructional coach*

"Never stop asking students about what they're learning. There's no need to guess when we have people right in front of us who can give us the information."

*—6th grade teacher*

# 6

# Assessment

*"I'm so stressed out," Felicia says to her colleague Tim. "I feel like I'm on a hamster wheel every day with my teaching, just going in circles."*

*"I've been there," he says. "Maybe I can help?"*

*"Really?" Felicia asks. "Because I've never seen you frazzled or wondering what's coming next."*

*"Well, no," Tim agrees, "because you didn't know me at the point in my career when I was barely getting by. I've learned how to do more by focusing on fewer things. I realize that sounds vague."*

*"Can you give me an example?"*

*Tim thinks for a minute. "OK, I've got something. So, you know how any given unit has a pretty big group of standards we're supposed to teach?"*

*"Indeed I do," Felicia says, rolling her eyes.*

*"Well, it used to really intimidate me. I didn't know what to do, or when, or how much. But then I realized it was about sequencing and prioritizing. I can't teach all the standards in one week. The most I could probably do and maintain any kind of clarity is two. So I mapped out all of them, looked at the substandards that support the larger anchor standards, and figured out how to lay them out in a way that was logical for the entire unit. That was step one."*

*"That sounds like so much, though," Felicia says. "I thought you said this would be easier."*

*"It didn't take that long, and I did it with my teammates," Tim explains. "We set aside a couple of planning periods to really look at what we were doing, and we did it well in advance. We also decided to simplify things by developing an instructional approach that structured each week in a specific way."*

*"What does that mean?"*

*"In this case, we used Monday and Wednesday for direct instruction, Tuesday and Wednesday for choice-based workdays, and Friday to check in with kids and do something a little more fun, like a learning game."*

*"What's a learning game?" Felicia asks.*

*Tim smiles. "Here, I'll show you." He pulls out his laptop.*

◀————————▶

Too often, teachers feel as though they are spinning in circles. However, it is possible to be discerning by narrowing down a wider repertoire of teaching moves in order to serve students to the maximum benefit. In the scenario just related, Tim champions a "less is more" approach to teaching by setting up a weekly structure that combines a variety of instructional modes and gives him the time and space to work with students in different ways. To simplify a hectic teaching life, remember to establish the strong habits that address instructional approach and that are discussed in the preceding chapters—habits such as the following:

- Determine learning priorities and nonnegotiables as early in the planning process as possible.
- Analyze the root causes of difficulty with classroom management.
- Be surgical with data analysis to ensure that students are focused on the skills that will help them the most.
- Work with the goal of creating a deeper level of cognitive engagement.

When teachers focus on the instructional priorities that most clearly support desired learning targets, student success becomes apparent through aligned, measurable assessment data. Admittedly, *assessment* is one of the most highly charged words in education, one of those terms that tends to get knee-jerk responses that are tinged with inaccurate perceptions (like *vaccine* in medicine and *damages* in legal circles). Like any word that takes on implications that go beyond technical meaning, it is challenging to so much as utter anything about assessment (particularly if it is standardized or mandated) without having people weigh in with strong opinions. However, as is the case with many words that evolve over time to take on different associations, assessment itself gets an often undeserved bad rap.

## Addressing the Stigma

In its truest form, assessment is intended to measure student growth toward specific content standards. However, logistical or practical roadblocks frequently interfere with data analysis. Most notably, a lack of timeliness or transparency can prevent teachers from applying what they learn from student performance quickly enough for it to be of any help. Veteran educators Stephen Chappuis and Jan Chappuis (2012) affirm that "the results may not be communicated in ways that teachers and students can easily interpret and work with. Further, the results are often delivered months after the administration of the tests" (p. 2). Therefore, it is up to school and district leaders to ensure that the quick turnaround of testing data is a high priority.

When administered correctly and analyzed surgically, assessments provide key information that guides instruction as teachers determine what students know and what they have yet to learn. Rather than go down the rabbit hole of debate over standardized exams and their application to classroom content, it is far more productive to ensure the wisest use of assessment within anyone's given circle of control. Whether that translates to school districts creating unit tests that align to curriculum standards or individual teaching teams developing formative determinants of student success, the process of uncovering what students need is one that should be implemented with care.

With assessment design, the process moves more smoothly when content is prioritized over shallow considerations, such as length. A test need not be long or cumbersome to capture necessary information, nor does an assignment need to be graded with endless strings of comments for a teacher to determine next steps. Think about how the following "habit stack" could make assessment more doable:

1. Pick one skill as an assessment focus based on observations or data that indicate potential areas of student struggle.
2. Build a short formative assessment to measure that skill with the intention of providing feedback rather than a grade.
3. Sort students into holistic categories of "Met" and "Not Yet."
4. Record any patterns that appear.
5. Share patterns with students and explain next instructional steps.
6. Once student needs have been addressed, administer an assessment that goes beyond feedback to provide a grade.

To help students make progress, administering a series of long assessments is not just cumbersome but usually unnecessary. Sometimes less is more. Building the habit of putting intention behind the skills that students are asked to demonstrate with efficiency is a key step in removing the stigma associated with assessment.

## Getting a Snapshot

When most people think of testing, they envision students struggling through a challenging hour, or teachers grading into the night. The traditional use of assessment can certainly be arduous, but the pain that everyone pictures doesn't have to be a constant reality.

Chapter 3 explored the importance of backward design in planning so that when teachers assess students, the evidence they gather is matched to the right standard of focus for learning. However, once an assessment is given, the data must be interpreted in a way that determines effective next steps. For many teachers, this process is associated with hours of grading papers or writing detailed feedback for students, only to see rubrics or comments wind up being disregarded. Naturally, it gets frustrating to see all the work that goes into grading fail to achieve its intended purpose of helping students achieve growth.

Because everyone knows that doing the same thing repeatedly and expecting different results is a futile pursuit, it helps to reframe the process of grading and analysis in a more direct, doable way. Just as students need a clear list of criteria for success to be able to reach their learning target—criteria expressed in language they fully understand rather than in complex "edujargon"—teachers benefit from an equally clear method for interpreting student performance data.

To explore the idea of doing less to achieve more by simplifying the assessment process, Figure 6.1 is one example of a quick, efficient way to gather information about what students know. This sorting tool is highly precise in that the teacher identifies a clear objective for what students need to learn. Rather than spending time writing extended commentary or working on individual papers, the teacher makes three piles: "exceeds standard," "meets standard," and "not yet." As the teacher reads student work, he is also on the lookout for patterns that appear across the class, especially in each category. That way, he can record observations in the "notes" section and use that information to guide what happens next.

Perhaps not every assessment can be graded with the efficiency of the sorting tool, but many of them can, which removes the endless frustration of spending so much time grading work that students might not even look at. Even more important, the patterns that emerge from

**Figure 6.1.  Sorting Tool**

| **Helpful Habit:** *Sort students into groups related to achievement of an identified learning target.* | | | |
|---|---|---|---|
| | **Exceeds Standard** | **Meets Standard** | **Not Yet** |
| *Objective* <br> Students will be able to identify two specific traits that describe the central character. | 4 | 18 | 8 |
| *Notes* | Students either described more than two traits or went into further detail/ depth about their observations. | The students in this group identified two traits. They did not go beyond the task or think profoundly about character. | Students identified one trait in many cases rather than two. The rest summarized instead of selecting traits. |

sorting student achievement into groups can help guide instruction on a particular objective. If just a few students are in the "not yet" category, for example, the teacher can work with them individually to help scaffold progress toward the desired result. However, when a larger group of students demonstrates the struggle of "not yet," that may indicate further instruction still needs to be accomplished in a whole-group setting.

Although it can be counterintuitive for many teachers who are accustomed to laboring for long hours over student work to streamline their methods by doing less, getting a snapshot of progress is highly informative. It also clarifies the details of where holistic student struggle lies and prevents anyone from getting too far into the weeds of inconsequential, and possibly distracting, details (such as minor errors) in individual student papers. There is no rule that the process of interpreting assessments has to be long and painful, though that is certainly the perception. Instead, working smarter and not harder provides better results that teachers can appreciate and apply to their analysis of student work.

## Short and Quick

Over the past several years, formative approaches have gained significant traction as a preferred method of assessment, thanks in large part to the ideology behind the practice. Not too long ago, students were taught material in classrooms, mainly via stand-and-deliver direct instruction, and were subsequently asked to demonstrate their learning in what is now called a summative or "high-stakes" assessment. In this model, it wasn't just grades that were cast in stone once test results came back; there was also an assumption that students knew the material enough to move forward with new concepts and that anyone who was falling behind needed to either catch up or succumb to continued (perhaps permanent) struggle.

This sink-or-swim approach to education has lost popularity over time, particularly in the wake of both increased awareness of equity-driven instruction and amid the aftereffects of teaching and learning during the pandemic. Turning a blind eye to student struggle is harmful, and so is closing down opportunities for growth. Additionally, the idea of determining student achievement within any given content standard only at the close of a unit of instruction is fundamentally unsound. Ideally, teachers clear up confusion and check for understanding continuously throughout a unit of study.

The pushback that leaders often encounter when they ask teachers to formatively assess students with more frequency is centered on a protectiveness around two rare commodities: time and bandwidth. How, teachers ask, can they possibly assess students with any frequency when the instructional period is short, when grading piles up, and when district leaders provide no extra time for planning or preparation?

The answer to a complex question can be startlingly simple, and that is true in this instance. Rather than think of formative assessment as a drawn-out process, it helps to focus on using tools that will tell us what we need to know quickly. Like the sorting tool featured in Figure 6.1, the following assessment bank shares some tried-and-true methods of quickly gathering information about what students know and are able to do. Students can be asked to do any of the following:

- Take a brief poll (one or two questions).
- Summarize the daily learning goal in one sentence.
- Fill out an exit or entry ticket that shares a concept or presents an open-ended question.
- Hold up color-coded cards (often red, yellow, and green to align with traffic lights) to indicate a level of understanding or confusion.
- Reflect briefly (3–5 sentences) about a concept.
- Complete the sentence stem: "I still don't understand . . . ."
- Place questions that don't need immediate attention into a communal "Parking Lot."
- Put "Burning Questions" on the board to clear up more immediate confusion.
- Draw an important concept instead of writing about it.
- Take new learning and apply it to a different situation.
- Create a short assessment for peers to complete.
- Write a brief social media–style summary of the learning.
- Make a "mic drop" statement that leaves everyone with a final thought for the day, either orally or in writing.

When students complete brief assessment activities like these, they more clearly focus on the outcome of whatever they learned, and their progress is also more visible. Shorter checks for understanding do not negate the need for longer, summative tests that show what students have learned by the close of a unit or a period of study. However, when teachers grow weary of giving one long assessment after another with dubious benefits, adopting the regular habit of using quick formatives removes a great deal of stress and uncovers valuable data that moves everyone in the classroom forward.

## Making Adjustments

*"Wow," Mr. Jasper says, looking at his online gradebook. "They did so much better with this exit ticket."*

*Lindy, his teammate, leans over to look at his screen. "Which one was that?"*

*"The one where they had to ask an open-ended question about the function of some additional bones we learned about. I have a student named Kylie who wasn't as engaged with the content as she seemed, which made me wonder about the other kids. I designed some shorter summarizers to formatively assess what everyone actually knows before they leave a classroom."*

*Lindy nods. "I've often had that experience, too. I think kids know something, but then they throw me for a loop when they take a test. I've been trying to do more formatives also. They just take a lot of time."*

*"Not these," Mr. Jasper says. "I've been experimenting with much shorter checks for understanding, and I also don't always grade everything. Instead, I sort the kids into groups according to what they seem to be comprehending. Almost all the time, the kids who are making mistakes have things in common, so I can address it with them in my teaching before they take a test for a grade."*

*"And it really saves time?"*

*"Yes, because I'm not reteaching everything. When I was doing things the old way, I was in a constant loop of teaching and reteaching. Now, with these shorter exit tickets, I have a better sense of what's happening with*

*kids more consistently. Plus, they're more engaged because they have so much more understanding of what we're doing."*

*"Can you share some of your favorite shorter assessments with me?"*

*"You bet," Mr. Jasper says, looking through his exit tickets once more. He's so pleased with everyone's progress, and he knows he can keep things going in the right direction.*

When teachers use intuition to determine where student learning stands, they can be incorrect about their assumptions, at least in part. The same holds true in classrooms where students are only assessed in formal ways, as opposed to experiencing regular informal measures that show a complete picture of growth over time. Adjusting practice is not something that occurs all at once or in a noticeable way. Rather, the finer details of assessment are layered gradually to produce more lasting change.

To apply the principles of habit stacking to increase the use of quicker and more incisive assessment measures, think about a progression that occurs in minute steps. The first step might be picking just one day a week to administer a formative assessment to students. The second step could center on designing a very short assessment to hand out. Step three would be to actually try out the process with students once the pieces are in place, and step four could involve using the sorting tool (or a similar method) to gather data. This process might take a couple of weeks to get off the ground, which is fine. There is no race to the finish when we think about improving pedagogy. As one assessment format becomes comfortable, more can be added: another day to check for understanding, another formative technique to try, and so forth. Slowly, it will become second nature to incorporate small but powerful assessments regularly into practice and analyze the results.

Change takes effort and time, but that doesn't mean everything needs to happen all at once. Instead, by invoking the spirit of the well-known fable of the tortoise and hare, slower and steadier will gradually ensure that the word *assessment* finally loses the infamous stigma it has accrued over so many years and begins to take on a new, better meaning all its own.

## Tiny Teaching Tips: Assessment

"Do an assessment of their work against the criteria for success. Look for patterns. Then, stop the group while they are working and provide targeted feedback and support."

*—John Jeffries, retired teacher*

"Know what you're looking for long before you ever teach anybody anything."

*—10th grade geometry teacher*

# AFTER INSTRUCTION

When any unit of instruction concludes, a natural reaction is to forge ahead with whatever comes next, both for the sake of pacing and for the relief of doing something new. But however tempting it might be to imagine that a subsequent learning focus signifies a fresh start, any "been there, done that" thinking about content outcomes has strong limitations. Teaching and learning do not consist of discrete sets of experiences, and the goal is not to "get through" curriculum by prioritizing pacing. Rather, identifying and maintaining emphasis on instructional through lines is essential in helping students understand the connections that exist not just during one year of study, but also in their future learning. To that end, teachers must provide students with the information they need to correctly analyze and reflect upon the reasons for their academic achievement so that they have continuous, accurate knowledge about where they stand.

# Feedback, Guidance, and Evaluation

*"I'm handing back your unit tests," Ms. Sanders says. "As you'll see, the results were not what I was hoping for."*

*The room is completely silent as one by one, students get their papers back. Taking advantage of the quiet, Ms. Sanders goes to the front of the room. "To be honest, I'm just as upset by these scores as you must be, if not more. I thought we talked about the importance of studying, and now I'm not sure anyone was listening."*

*Melanie has been looking at her paper in dismay, and what Ms. Sanders says bothers her enough that she speaks without raising her hand. "That's not true," Melanie objects. "I feel like we were listening. I studied the vocabulary you told us to focus on and reread all the handouts. The test had some of that, but I didn't realize there would be other things on it, too."*

*"Those are concepts from earlier in the year," Ms. Sanders says. "The test is cumulative. You learned some of the words and information months ago."*

*"I don't know about anyone else, but I forgot them. You never said we had to study those, too. I just studied what was in the unit."*

*"Yeah," chimes in Oscar, who sits behind Melanie. "Same here. Our review quiz was just about those words, too. Why didn't you say you were going to test us on everything?"*

*Ms. Sanders is miffed. "When you take this class, anything you learn could appear on a test. I didn't think I needed to explain that."*

*"Well, you did," Melanie says. "Otherwise, it feels like a trick. I could have studied these other words, too. I just forgot them, since we haven't used them in months. It's not fair."*

*"I agree," says another student in the back row. "Why did you have us do all these review activities if they didn't matter?"*

*Ms. Sanders doesn't know what to say. Secretly, she wonders if her students are right, but years of teaching this way make her inclined to dig in her heels. Maybe what she did needs to be reexamined, but she doesn't know any other way to teach.*

## Starting Backward to Move Forward

Effective teaching necessitates a great deal of forethought. If we look at student success as a destination, feedback should be designed to point kids toward a clearly identified end goal. Otherwise, it's like getting on the road to drive to an unfamiliar town without a map; if we happen to make it to the right place, it's accidental. Teachers never want student outcomes to be guided by luck, nor do they usually intend to make the keys to learning opaque. However, more frequently than desired, students do not understand what they need to do to improve their outcomes, and unfortunately that also means that sometimes, neither do their teachers.

In Chapter 3, I highlighted the process of backward design to emphasize that before any instruction can occur, two things need to happen: teachers must (1) establish a learning goal and (2) determine the evidence that will demonstrate whether students have reached the desired target. As the most crucial part of that second step of backward design, the importance of delivering feedback that clearly explains performance to students cannot be emphasized enough. However, when the time comes to design feedback processes, teachers may wind up inadvertently creating more confusion, for both themselves and their students. Think about a fairly common scenario: a teacher grading papers. For the past few days, this teacher's class has been working on looking for the main idea in a passage. The teacher has guided the students in practicing this skill with a few passages and then has administered a formative assessment that asks them to look at three short passages and identify the central point of each one. As the teacher looks through the papers, she feels annoyed because students consistently identify the main idea incorrectly; many of them are focusing on smaller details, and some have missed the message completely.

At this point, many teachers rely on intuition, conclude that their students haven't achieved the desired outcome, and attribute this lack of success to factors such as inattention or capacity. Although this causal attribution might be correct, it could also be wildly inaccurate, especially if the assessment did not clearly isolate the skill of pulling out the main idea of a passage. Perhaps the passages themselves were tough to interpret and full of distracters; maybe students only understood the main idea when they had the guidance of a teacher and they needed more time to practice on their own. It might also be possible that although students were able to isolate the main idea of some passages, the ones on the assessment were not geared toward the correct grade-level content standard.

Several possibilities could explain why students might not be performing as expected, and the only way that a teacher can discover for certain what went wrong would be to do two things: (1) refine the pieces of backward design to ensure the most accurate assessment measures possible and (2) have a feedback process that is focused on specific, transparent criteria that students are explicitly aware they must meet. To begin the habit of providing feedback designed to uncover student knowledge, beginning with one tiny but important detail—knowing the true meaning of what feedback is meant to be—paves the way for a more effective process.

## Feedback: Getting It Right

When people talk about giving one another feedback, they often misuse the term. Suppose a child is learning ballet and the teacher says, "Pull back your shoulders." The teacher thinks that she has just provided important feedback about posture, but to the student, it might just come across as a random directive rather than a piece of information that will lead to greater overall success in dance, which is a medium that relies on body positioning and proprioception, an awareness of the various body parts and how they move. Because feedback is so often misconstrued, teachers must allow students a more active role in how it is designed so that everyone understands its purpose.

To ensure that feedback works better for everyone, the language of assessment needs to be much clearer. As Grant Wiggins (2012) affirms, "The term feedback is often used to describe all kinds of comments made after the fact, including advice, praise, and evaluation. But none of these are feedback, strictly speaking." For many teachers, this idea is befuddling at the outset. After years of writing comments on papers, assigning grades, and giving students wise counsel, they wonder, how could any (or perhaps all) of that hard work not be classified as feedback?

Uncovering the difference between feedback and what Wiggins refers to as "advice, praise, and evaluation" begins with one idea: objectivity. Suppose a teacher regularly arrives at work about 10 minutes into his first-period class, causing the department chair to cover his class each time the late arrival occurs. If the department chair says to the teacher, "You are arriving late to work several times a week," that is an objective observation that acts as feedback about when the teacher is arriving in relation to the expectation of timeliness. However, if the department chair says, "You need to leave your house 10 minutes earlier," that is guidance. And of course, if a performance review is written up to report this regular infraction, that is a form of evaluation. Feedback, however, just lets people know where they stand in relation to an expected standard. As Wiggins (2012) states, "Basically, feedback is information about how we are doing in our efforts to reach a goal."

When feedback is provided correctly, the focus is on what people are *doing,* not who they *are.* For students, this distinction is critically important. So many kids feel judged in school spaces, particularly by their teachers. When they understand what is expected of them with coursework and feedback is closely aligned with those expectations, they stop feeling as though being successful in class is a personal game of chance. Furthermore, the transparent objectivity of a correctly executed feedback process reduces the likelihood of bias creeping into the equation, an important consideration for students who experience regular marginalization. For the teacher, focusing on criteria for success provides a "less is more" approach that negates the unproductive habit of spending hours on grading student work.

To remove the stigma of assessment being anything but impartial, teachers and students must first understand the difference between a grading rubric and criteria for success. At first glance, the snippet in Figure 7.1 looks like one row of a typical holistic rubric that works on a four-point scale. However, the column under number 4 has been shaded to emphasize an important point. When teachers share criteria for success with students, those criteria are represented in the topmost point on a rubric. If instruction has been carried out with transparency, students have seen a list of criteria for success for each assignment they receive at the outset. Then, when the rubric is handed back for evaluative purposes, they more fully understand which criteria they met (thus, the score of 4 indicates fully meeting the standard) and what they need to improve on.

Suppose a student who has received a score of 3 on the rubric sample in Figure 7.1 is trying to understand why she did not get the highest grade possible. As she looks at the rubric, this student should be able to cross-reference her score (an evaluative measure) with the criteria for success that the teacher listed on the initial assignment. *Oh,* this student thinks. *It looks like I only answered part of one of the questions. I see what happened.* In this case, the teacher has provided objective feedback about how this student performed in relation to an identified target. The

**Figure 7.1. Rubric and Criteria for Success**

| Helpful Habit: *Show students how criteria for success define the highest point on a rubric.* | | | | |
|---|---|---|---|---|
| **Criteria for Success** | **4** | **3** | **2** | **1** |
| The product answers three out of five questions fully and correctly. | The student has answered at least three questions fully and correctly. | The student has answered at least three questions, but one or more responses are incomplete or incorrect. | The student has answered fewer than three questions, and not all responses are complete or correct. | The student has answered fewer than three questions, and all responses are incomplete or incorrect. |

student realizes she came up a little short of that target and that she needs to make adjustments to reach a score of 4 on this particular assessment.

Getting students to understand the value of how criteria for success fit into feedback requires a gradual approach. To "habit stack" this objective feedback process, consider the following steps:

1. Identify a specific skill or standard that an assignment will measure.
2. Create a list of criteria for success in student-friendly language that aligns with the chosen skill.
3. Explicitly share and explain both the skill focus and the criteria list with students at the start of an assignment.
4. If using a rubric, ensure that the highest score on the rubric aligns with the criteria for success.
5. When assessing student work, use the list of criteria for success as a starting point for objective feedback.

Students who receive judgment-free feedback can focus on what they have produced rather than become mired in the possibility that grading systems are based on unfair and hidden criteria, such as who the teacher likes. That way, a class can be seen as an equitable playing field rather than a tricky obstacle course to figure out. When students no longer feel resentment or fear, they become far more open to receiving suggestions from teachers that will improve their performance.

## Guidance and Evaluation

*"OK, folks," Ms. Sanders announces. "Time to hand back the test. What do we remember about getting our grades back?"*

*Melanie responds, "No comparing our papers with one another."*

*"And we're not trying to be perfect. We're working on getting better," another student adds.*

*Ms. Sanders smiles. "Great start. Anything else?"*

*There is a pause as everyone in the room tries to remember what they are told whenever any kind of assessment is returned. Suddenly, Oscar shoots his hand into the air and talks at the same time. "Oh! I know! We should look at that list thing on the last page to figure out what we did wrong before we ask you."*

*"The criteria for success," Ms. Sanders says. "And it's not necessarily what you did wrong. We're looking for areas of improvement. OK?"*

*As everyone nods and murmurs, Ms. Sanders makes her way around the room to hand back the tests, watching students carefully as she goes. She knows that the year got off to a bumpy start and that her students didn't trust her, and she has worked hard to change the way she assesses their work so that there is a "no secrets" approach to tests and students know what is expected of them. Before she made these changes, kids wouldn't just get angry at her every time she returned a test. They would also immediately start talking to one another about their scores. Instead of reading through her comments, they also wanted her to talk about the grade right away. But now, several months later, Ms. Sanders no longer faces that reaction. The change is the result of a consistent system of feedback that helps students understand what they are supposed to be learning in preparation for the assessment and see where they might have made mistakes based on clear criteria for success that are shared throughout the process.*

*Sure enough, kids are quietly looking through their papers, focusing not just on the grade but also on what might be missing based on the criteria for success. When a box isn't checked off as meeting the standard, Ms. Sanders writes a brief note to explain what the student can do to fix the issue.*

*After a few minutes, Oscar looks up and whispers, "Are we allowed to talk yet?"*

*Ms. Sanders laughs. "You can come up here and ask me a question if you've looked through everything."*

*Oscar gets up and approaches her. "I totally understand what I missed," he says. "I just wanted to know if you have time at lunch to help me, because I already knew I didn't get this part. I just haven't figured out how to do it yet."*

*"Absolutely," Ms. Sanders says. "And great use of growth-mindset language there too."*

*"Thanks," Oscar says. He returns to his seat, and Ms. Sanders briefly reflects on how far their relationship has come before she begins moving around the room to check on other students.*

In functional classrooms, students understand what they need to do to be successful. To make things clearer for everyone, the language of feedback, guidance, and evaluation can be contextualized with parallels to something all of us have experienced: food. Imagine a budding cook (say, a teenager) who has decided to make omelets for his family. Despite his best intentions, the end product is rubbery and bland. The teenager knows that omelets aren't supposed to taste like this; he has had plenty in his life that are light, fluffy, and bursting with flavor. Something must be wrong, but he is uncertain of what he did to achieve such a poor result. If someone in his house is knowledgeable, that person can provide feedback on the quality of the dish by objectively sharing what was missing. However, it would also be helpful to give the teenager guidance for the future. Perhaps he should adjust the cooking heat, add more seasoning, or take the omelet pan off the burner sooner. But unless he is trying to replicate a restaurant review experience, probably nobody in his family should evaluate his performance.

People learn through trial and error, but as criteria for success indicate, everyone needs a visible target. Though students cannot know how to improve their work without feedback, they also need guidance to make progress. Otherwise they may not see what changes they can make to progress to the next level. Therefore, teachers can and should provide explicit suggestions for improvement that tie into identified criteria for success. That way, rather than facing holistic comments that are often unhelpful and difficult to interpret in terms of where to begin, students know exactly what needs their attention to move to a higher level of achievement. To that end, here are some examples of guidance statements that provide focus for students across grade levels and content areas:

- Try making a straighter line for your letter *D* so that it doesn't get mistaken for the letter *O*.
- To meet the criteria, add one more example from the text that demonstrates your point.
- If you look back over the problem, you'll see that you accidentally missed a step.

- Clearly label all parts of the cell in neat handwriting to make this easier to read.
- Look at the section of the chapter (page 35) that goes into more depth about the role of women during this time.
- Think about how to elaborate on these ideas a little more.
- When you are working, do your best to slow down and check your answers.
- Remember to capitalize the first word of every sentence.

Students typically appreciate clear, specific guidance that is geared toward a visible goal, but they feel differently about grades. When teachers seek to evaluate student performance, it usually takes the form of a letter or a number. Often considered a necessary evil, grades are an extrinsic motivator designed to create accountability so that students are more likely to learn course objectives. Grades are also used (or abused, as the case may be) as a behavior management technique to increase compliance, which is why teachers sometimes assign scores for things like participation or cooperation. When students are evaluated for their behavior, the purpose of grades becomes opaque. Are they meant as an unbiased measure of progress, or are they an arbitrary value placed on subjective factors that might have nothing to do with achievement?

There are many reasons why evaluating students can become a minefield, so it is incredibly important to remove as many obstacles as possible to the intended function of grades. Not only should grades not bear any connection to behavior, but they should also accurately measure where student performance sits in relation to a specific set of content standards. A rubric that is set up like the one in Figure 7.1 illustrates why aligning grades closely with criteria for success is the ideal way to achieve an evaluation system that makes sense to everyone. For students, it is just as crucial to understand grading systems and point values as it is for their teachers. Otherwise, the process of evaluation becomes one more barrier to possible success, and many students simply give up when they perceive that the process is unfair.

Getting the balance right among feedback, guidance, and evaluation might not be easy at the outset, but it is an endeavor well worth taking on. As teachers slowly build habits toward improving this process, it becomes easier to help students understand their own progress. Consider criteria for success as a starting point for better feedback. Suppose we resolve to include a list of student-friendly, clear criteria with every single assignment. Once that becomes commonplace and everyone understands the process, moving on to more specific guidance is a clear next step. Then, rubrics or evaluation measures can be tweaked to include the criteria for success as a natural step of grading. Eventually, students will finally understand how to be successful and feel empowered in their ability to guide their own academic futures.

### Tiny Teaching Tips: Feedback, Guidance, and Evaluation

"If I don't give my students any indication of what I expect before they do an assignment, I'm setting everyone up for frustration. I include myself in that."

*—11th grade teacher*

"The more concrete I can be with suggestions, the more useful my guidance becomes."

*—Music education teacher*

# 8

# Analysis and Reflection

*"Ugh, not another data meeting," Nico says as he sits down. "It doesn't matter how many times we talk about why kids are failing. Nothing is going to change."*

*Across the table, Jess glances at him. "You'd better not let the higher-ups hear you talk like that."*

*"I almost don't care anymore. Nobody can fix the fact that, like it or not, kids won't do the work. How am I supposed to talk about data we don't have? A zero is literally a nonexistent data point if we're trying to figure out what kids know."*

*"Doesn't it depend on why they got a zero?"*

*"Come on," Nico says. "You and I both know that if a kid tries to do any work at all, we'll give them some kind of credit. A zero means we never saw anything happen."*

*"I mean, why didn't it happen?" Jess persists. "Was it because they were absent? Or were they literally sitting in class and doing nothing?"*

*"Some of the time, they're not there. But," Nico admits, "there are times the kids just sit there. I don't usually go overboard trying to make them work. That's a power struggle, which never helps."*

*"Yeah, but then we still get blamed. A kid was there, not working. We let it be, and now there's an absence of data."*

*Before Nico can reply, their assistant principal walks in. "Hey," Rita says, sitting down. "Are we good to go?"*

*Nico and Jess exchange a quick glance, and Rita notices it. "Or . . . maybe we're not?" she guesses.*

*"It's not that," Jess says. "We were just talking about how frustrating these data chats can be. It feels like we're spinning in circles. The problem never really seems to change or get better."*

*Rita has been a school leader for a long time, and she knows better than to jump into a tricky conversation too early. Sure enough, she waits a few beats and Nico speaks up.*

*"It's not that I like what's happening," he says, "but the kids keep failing because they don't even attempt the work. How can I assess that? How can any of us make improvements when students won't give us the bare minimum?" He points to his grade book, which displays a confetti-like pattern of one zero after another.*

*Without looking at the grades, Rita says, "I understand your point. You want data, and you feel that there's not much to work with. That must be frustrating."*

*"It is," Nico says, the color in his cheeks heightening. "And I don't see the point of talking it to death."*

*"But," Rita continues as though he hasn't spoken, "there is a purpose to analyzing even what isn't there in the hopes that we can develop some actions toward change. What have you done so far?"*

*Jess breaks in. "It's not that we haven't tried things. I just wonder whether we're missing some piece of the puzzle. Short of locking kids in the rooms until they do the work, it's hard to force them to do something."*

*Rita sits back and thinks. She doesn't want to keep repeating herself, and she also isn't sure what should happen next. The reasons behind why students don't complete their work, even with encouragement or incentives, remain unclear. Like the teaching team in front of her, Rita is at a loss. Maybe data meetings aren't a good idea until the team figures out how to find whatever they're looking for. But where to start?*

◄ ――――― ►

The situation that Nico and Jess find themselves confronting is far from unusual. The process of gathering and analyzing student data is rife with difficulty. How do we know that a root-cause analysis is accurate and that appropriate solutions are being developed to move kids forward? Without finely tuned processes and attention to the right details, both teachers and leaders can spend months (if not years) chasing the wrong approaches to whatever challenges present themselves consistently. To make way for a new reality, unscrambling the confusion around gathering data is essential if we want to avoid the classic trap of doing the same thing repeatedly and expecting, through some miracle or other, different results.

## Correlation, Causation, Confusion

In late 2022, I made a guest appearance on a podcast to talk about one of my books. As I was chatting with the host, he posed a question I wasn't expecting: "In the wake of the pandemic, why are so many kids still showing significant lapses in appropriate behavior? Why are the kids not all right?"

Why, indeed.

As I answered the podcaster's question, I led with a disclaimer that felt important to denote. We were, I explained, at the start of a time in which student behavior (and adult behavior, to be frank) had dramatically shifted as a result of global trauma. Any assumptions I held about the root cause of this shift would be guesswork, but time would tell a more complete story. My theory was and continues to be that children stopped trusting heretofore reliable adults (including teachers) during 2020 and 2021 because those adults suddenly seemed to have no clear idea of what steps would get everyone safely through a crisis. Still, I had no significant evidence other than some anecdotal data that could prove my conjecture to be even partly true—or, beyond that, applicable to a wider swath of the population. It might be 20 years or more before we really have a sense of how the pandemic shaped schools in the time that followed.

School leaders don't have the luxury of waiting 20 years to figure out how to help kids, and teachers have even less time. Most students sit in a teacher's classroom for anywhere from 5 to 10 months, and then our time with them is up. How can root-cause analysis be conducted accurately, meaningfully, and in a way that really helps students achieve growth?

The first step to analyzing data correctly is to be cognizant of how necessary it is to remove bias from the equation. Otherwise, our brains create links between events and their causes that are misaligned. As business professor Michael Luca (2021) points out, "A large body of research in behavioral economics and psychology has highlighted systematic mistakes we can make when looking at data. We tend to seek evidence that confirms our preconceived notions and ignore data that might go against our hypotheses" (para. 3). It's human nature to want to verify what we already believe. For example, researchers have tried to establish a link between diet soda consumption and weight gain for a long time. However, their studies have been done with relatively small sample groups and usually with adults who have several inadvisable health habits or preexisting conditions. Therefore, news headlines that imply a connection between artificially sweetened beverages and obesity may be biased and flawed.

The same complications related to faulty application of root-cause analysis run rampant in schools that have weaker systems around professional learning on the topic of analysis and reflection. Whether students are successful in reaching learning targets or struggling, the ways in which teachers attribute performance can be incorrect if the data interpretation process is overly subjective or if a lack of information leads to making assumptions rather than analyzing measurable indicators of growth.

To allay confusion over where the cause of struggle truly lies, building strategies to engage in a surgical analysis of student performance is key to solving the right problems, as well as to not disturbing systems that are working just fine. Consider implementing any of the following habits to make the process of data analysis more meaningful:

1. Determine a narrow focus for each assignment by targeting just one specific skill for analysis rather than several.
2. Remain open to the possibility that students may perform unexpectedly with the selected skill, and be prepared to change course as needed.
3. Make criteria for success as value-free and objective as possible.

When we challenge our own thinking around why students are performing in a particular way and leave possibilities more open, we expend less energy on going down pathways that may or may not yield desired results. Furthermore, once everyone perceives the benefit of diagnosing student data correctly after seeing positive shifts in student work, they will be less likely to rely on intuition to make instructional decisions.

# Removing Distracters

When we try to figure out why students aren't reaching a learning target, it becomes all too easy to focus on the wrong thing by looking at either one piece of student data or a single portion of an assessment. To check this tendency, education consultant Daniel R. Venables (2014) suggests that we ask these questions: "So what does this imply for all of our students? What general observations do you have that affect most of our students? Do you think this is representative of all students [or all test items]?" (p. 141). That way, the conversation becomes focused on overall patterns rather than on individual outliers.

In addition, although it can be difficult to resist the urge to form conclusions that seem to emerge clearly, remembering our inherent bias and giving the analytical process more time is key to removing distractions from student data. If performance on a given task is lower than expected, for example, many teachers will decide on several steps for mitigation right away. Instead, in the interest of not going in an ultimately futile direction, it makes more sense to gather additional information from students about their assessment experiences to better understand what happened and how much the data reflect an isolated set of circumstances as opposed to a situation that needs further instruction. Otherwise we risk reteaching concepts that need no further emphasis and ignoring the genuine reasons behind the struggle. The following "habit stacks" can increase our effectiveness in removing distracters to student success, from bias to underlying assumptions:

- Examine evidence of student progress as objectively as possible; try not to look for something that is not clearly there.
- To help eliminate bias, consider looking at all student work without names attached.
- Brainstorm possible root causes for struggle by writing down all possibilities that come to mind, not just the more obvious or convenient ideas.

To implement a data analysis and reflection process that removes distracters from the equation, we once again turn to the tiny yet crucial details of what students experience. That way, any processes we build around determining where the next steps of instruction lie are housed in incisive habits that link correlation and causation accurately.

## Details of Growth

Throughout this book, we've embraced the idea that the devil (or in this case, the solution) lies in the details of instruction. Regardless of grade level or content area, narrowing the focus on student performance to a specific skill or standard is a necessary part of being able to conduct any kind of accurate analysis. Otherwise, there are too many possible variables to look at. Consider, for example, how many different skill sets are involved in a student writing sample. Any given paragraph includes a number of possible factors that contribute to success or failure. If we see that a student is pulling out textual evidence that doesn't support an overall focus, that might seem like the problem. But what if that issue was an anomaly or perhaps a symptom of a different challenge, such as a larger misunderstanding of the task? It can be so hard to correctly diagnose what is really happening.

For that reason, data analysis must be conducted in a way that demonstrates a clearly productive outcome for students. Otherwise, the process becomes akin to the results of a Harvard study in which researchers "reviewed 23 student outcomes from 10 different data programs used in schools and found that the majority showed no benefits for students. Only two were positive for students and in one study, students were worse off" (Barshay, 2022). If endless rounds of data meetings produce no measurable gains (and perhaps even losses), how can teachers possibly buy into the process of measuring student growth with solid information as opposed to relying on gut instinct?

Gathering accurate information about students need not be a complicated process, but it must be focused. Assuming that instruction is clearly aligned to content standards, looking at data should be a natural next step. For example, the method of charting student growth featured in Figure 8.1 is a simple yet effective way to look at progress through the lens of an assignment that clearly supports a desired learning objective.

In Figure 8.1, the teacher has assigned a short writing task to measure student progress on Next Generation Science Standards (NGSS) in 4th grade. In addition, the teacher has cited a Common Core literacy standard for writing so that the method for how students are expressing their understanding of the NGSS is clear. Rather than just create a basic

## Figure 8.1. Toolbox Timesaver: Charting Student Growth

**Helpful Habit:** *For quick analysis, sort students into holistic groups by standard.*

**Focus Standard**

4-LS1-1: Construct an argument that plants and animals have internal and external structures that function to support survival, growth, behavior, and reproduction. (NGSS)

**Literacy Standard**

W.4.1: Write opinion pieces on topics or texts, supporting a point of view with reasons and information. (4-LS1-1)

| Student | Met | Not Yet |
| --- | --- | --- |
| Nathan | | ✓ |
| Angelo | ✓ | |
| Mya | ✓ | |
| Bri | | ✓ |
| Taylor | | ✓ |
| Nico | ✓ | |

**Notes**

- Half of the group is meeting the standard, and the other half is not.
- Of the three who met the standard, their paragraphs were correct but only used examples provided in class of internal/external structures (skin, heart, etc.).
- For those who are "not yet," two of three correctly identified either an internal or external structure, but not both.
- One of the "not yet" responses is an outlier. The response was only one sentence long and did not meet any criteria for success.

**Next Steps**

- Talk to Taylor to determine what happened. Attention? Understanding?
- Conduct a quick formative assessment where students work individually to list internal/external structures that have NOT been mentioned in class.
- Based on the results of the formative assessment, determine whether to proceed or conduct further instruction/assessment.

tally of who met the standard on the assessment and who did not, the teacher goes a little further. First, the "notes" section of the chart indicates possible patterns of performance in relation to expected criteria, and all the observations are objective. Then, in the "next steps" section, the teacher has developed a plan for how to attend to two specific issues that have emerged. The first is that one student has completed no specified criteria on the assessment, and the teacher will therefore speak to this student to figure out why that happened. For the remaining students, the teacher has a shorter activity planned that will formatively assess the root cause of any confusion.

The tool in Figure 8.1 demonstrates that properly determining the details of where student growth occurs (or remains stagnant) does not require long, onerous processes. Rather, the habit of focusing instruction on one skill at a time and breaking it into chunks is a more tenable way to figure out why students are performing a certain way. Still, even when confusion is removed from analysis and reflection, it can be difficult to find the time and space to think about how to proceed when students continue to struggle. Reflection time may be scarce in our current climate and culture, but there are smaller ways to become more efficient in giving better thought to how we design favorable conditions for student growth.

## The Luxury of Thought

During the summer months, teachers usually have sufficient time (barring working in summer school or other jobs) to consider fresh ideas, engage in professional development, and make plans for the upcoming school year. Once instruction gets underway, however, it becomes increasingly difficult to have the time to think about what to do when student learning falls short of where it needs to be. That is when having strong habits around reflection becomes paramount to successful outcomes.

Habit stacking is particularly helpful with reflection because just as our thinking is an internal process, so are the habits we develop over time. Establishing the norm of asking reflection questions at pivotal instructional moments begins with smaller steps. First, after each formative assessment opportunity, develop the practice of writing one reflective, open-ended question that comes from a place of genuine curiosity about how students performed. Once that habit has been in place for a few weeks, begin exploring possible answers to the questions. The next step is to look for patterns that emerge over the course of several pieces of student data, especially those that are connected to one or two related focus standards. Over time, being reflective becomes a natural step in the cycle of planning, instruction, and analysis. To get a sense of what a more structured reflective process looks like, Figure 8.2 presents an example of a possible method for not only aligning questions to standards and the assessments that support related learning objectives, but also delineating where student performance stands in relation to course outcomes.

In Figure 8.2, which extends the science class example in Figure 8.1, the teacher has organized the reflective process to ensure that questions around student success or struggle remain grounded in the focus standard (which guides the objective) and the measures of student progress that have been administered to determine where the class stands. That

**Figure 8.2.  Reflection Questions**

| |
| --- |
| **Helpful Habit:** *Organize the reflective process through open-ended questioning.* |
| **NGSS Standard: 4-LS1-1**<br><br>**Data Source(s)**<br>1. Student paragraph response on internal/external structures<br>2. Follow-up formative assessment: list of internal/external structures |
| **Student Success**<br>• What about the follow-up formative assessment opportunity helped to clarify expectations for students?<br>• With the paragraph response, what was unclear about the criteria for success? How can I avoid that issue in the future?<br>• How have I worked to uncover expectations for students while still holding them to the content standard?<br>• What have I learned about students in this unit that can better inform my planning moving forward?<br><br>**Student Struggle**<br>• For students who remain confused about the focus standard, what additional support would be most helpful?<br>• What barriers might apply not just to their understanding in this unit but also perhaps to their learning moving forward? |

way, any reflection is streamlined rather than vague and unproductive. Even better, the answers that the teacher develops to the questions are directly linked to the intended learning target and therefore more focused on objectively explaining student performance in reference to the desired standard.

Consider the teaching team of Nico and Jess from earlier in this chapter. What if they learn to implement the processes described in Figures 8.1 and 8.2? Their experience would look quite different.

◄———————►

*"Take a look at this," Nico says to Jess, pointing at his data-sorting table.*

*"What's that?"*

*"The kids did so well on this assessment. I was testing their knowledge of solving word problems with multiplication and division, and except for a couple of students, everyone knocked it out of the park."*

*"Do you know what happened with the ones who didn't?"*

*"I think so," Nico says. "In our previous unit, a lot more kids were struggling with the word problems themselves, so I focused a lot on deconstructing the language. I'm pretty sure the ones who are still not doing so well are having an issue with the math itself."*

*Jess holds out her hand. "Can I see?"*

*"Absolutely." Nico gives her the table, and Jess takes a look, reading the notes her teammate made to himself as he looked through the student responses.*

*When she's done, Jess nods. "I agree with what you're seeing. The students who got the problems wrong were going through the right process, except for this one kid right here. What's his deal?"*

*"Oh, that's Mikey," Nico says. "He's been absent a lot. I think if he were here, I'd have a better chance to help him with the concepts. I've talked to his dad in the past, so I think it's time to call again."*

*"Seems like it. But really," Jess says, "you should be so happy with these results. Remember how frustrated we used to get when we weren't sure why kids were failing?"*

*"I do, and I wouldn't go back there for the world," Nico says. "I used to think it was such a pain to isolate one standard every time I taught*

*something, but it really helps narrow the focus of where kids are. And honestly, sorting them into groups has become second nature. It just tells me so much more, and it's not that much more work."*

*"Tell Rita," Jess suggests.*

*"Our long-suffering assistant principal?" Nico jokes. "Maybe. But I wouldn't be telling her to toot my own horn. Maybe she can help teachers who are doing what we used to do."*

With all the demands that teachers face, finding ample time to analyze and reflect on student growth accurately and without bias can seem like a steep hill to climb. However, building the habit of focusing the results of student work on standards-based benchmarks for progress is a powerful way to remove distracters and other irrelevant details from our examination into the deeper root causes that are otherwise challenging to deconstruct. Then, moving into the next phase of instruction becomes a naturally cyclical progress as we explore the steps needed to close all unresolved loops and circle back to the intentional process of planning how to set up instruction for student success.

### Tiny Teaching Tips: Analysis and Reflection

"I can't tell you how many times I've been surprised that whatever I thought was wrong turned out to be something totally different. It's all about gathering a lot of different kinds of data."

*—3rd grade teacher*

"For me, reflecting on what happened during instruction is my favorite part. I get to be a detective."

*—Middle school EL teacher*

# Next Steps

Anyone who has taught for more than a few years can identify with the kind of cyclical weariness that comes with teaching. The loop seems endless: plan, teach, analyze, reflect, and go back to planning. Compounding the process is that with perhaps every new unit (and certainly with each new semester or school year), teachers face a bevy of fresh challenges related to meeting student needs. This constant push can feel repetitive, but remaining focused on how to best refine the process each time reinforces the fact that success is not an accident of good fortune but the result of focused intention.

For all teachers, habit stacking becomes especially important toward the end of each instructional cycle. If we do not hold ourselves to processes that allow all the pieces of planning, teaching, and analysis to move forward in a way that reflects what students need in real time, we risk stagnating growth. Taking small steps such as responding to just one piece of student feedback in a transparent way can begin a process that builds more trust in a classroom community and that in turn leads to better practices. Therefore, as we begin to draw the curtain on one unit or marking period to make way for the next, having the agility to make adjustments that are based on data rather than intuition makes each successive teaching and learning experience more worthwhile.

# Now What? Closing the Loop

*Uri studies the spreadsheet in front of him, frowning. No matter how many times he asks for student feedback, there is always at least one response that throws him a little.*

*For years, Uri has done the same long-term project with his class, usually with positive results. Students write a children's book over the course of a few weeks about a current event and then read their books aloud to one another. The stories range in both topic and tone, and kids usually get immersed in not just the content but also the process of creating the books themselves, whether they cut out pictures from magazines or do original artwork.*

*But now, Uri stares at a student comment he has never seen before. It reads, "This project felt really uncomfortable. I understand that some people like to be creative, but I would have preferred writing about my event and really going in depth. I don't get why we had to do this, other than the fact that it might have been some kind of opportunity to be 'fun.' You usually talk about options, but this time, it wasn't even brought up and I was afraid to ask."*

*After he's read the comment a few times, Uri crosses his arms and thinks. Although he has encountered some resistance over the years to the project, this is the first time that a student has been quite so emphatic. Usually kids are nervous about the artwork, and Uri makes sure to create criteria for success that are built around ideas and ingenuity rather than on aesthetics. All he asks is that everyone try as hard as they can to make a presentable product. But either he didn't do a good enough job of that, or perhaps this student wasn't ever convinced. The question is, what now?*

*The next day, Uri faces his class as they settle in for the period. "It's time for feedback on feedback," he says.*

*Uri's students are used to this process. After any big project or unit task, Uri gathers their thoughts and sifts through what worked for everyone and what needs improvement. He uses this time to explain both what he will change moving forward and what he cannot change, taking care to provide rationales for both.*

*When he gets to the comment that bothered him the day before, Uri is prepared. He has taken the time to consider the student's perspective, to remove his personal feelings from the equation, and to think about the objective need to do the project as a children's book. As he shares the paraphrased gist of the comment on a slide, Uri gets ready to explain why he is thinking of reconsidering aspects of the project while maintaining others, since it needs to meet a content skill that is about applying important themes to a variety of audiences to increase understanding of how people relate to cultural events.*

*"OK," he begins. "Let's talk about why this project was presented as a children's book. I know there are some strong feelings around that, and I want to validate those feelings. I also want to explain why this choice is so important to how we look at the world around us and how we help others to find meaning in events that can seem senseless or confusing."*

*Students are listening, and Uri takes a deep breath and continues, knowing that if he respects all points of view and explains where he's coming from, everything will be fine.*

◄────────►

Both adults and children resist the feedback process. We erase surveys without looking at them, roll our eyes at attempts to gather opinions, and disregard any results that are shared as being disingenuous. And really, who can blame us? Culture—both at large and in schools—is terribly fond of soliciting thoughts but not too keen on taking two important next steps: making the feedback visible to all and following up with actions. Part of the reason for this lack of transparency is that more times than anyone would like to acknowledge, surveys are not given in earnest because either decisions have been made already or there is no intention to alter the status quo. Most of us have likely thought something along the lines of "They aren't asking me for my opinion, not really. They just want to go through the motions."

Even when a feedback process appears to be genuine, the benefits of providing an opinion often don't seem to outweigh the drawbacks. For one thing, especially in schools, survey respondents are apprehensive about their comments (even those presented as anonymous) somehow being discovered, fearing that they will be held accountable for any points of dissension. Beyond that is the aforementioned lack of follow-through. Why bother responding to any kind of request for feedback if nothing ever seems to happen as a result? Instead, "habit stacking" the feedback-on-feedback process becomes crucial. Here is how to create this habit stack:

1. To start practicing feedback on feedback, ask students just one question. A good place to begin is "What is getting in the way of your learning?"
2. Read the feedback from students with as unbiased a lens as possible.
3. Specifically identify what can change and what needs to remain the same.
4. Develop a visual for students (a slide, a handout) that summarizes the feedback-on-feedback responses.
5. Share the summary clearly, openly, and with an open mind. Be sure to explain the rationale for making a change or for making no change at all.
6. The next time feedback on feedback is collected, ask one or two more questions to figure out what is working and what else students might have to say that has gone unasked.

In the previous scenario, Uri has a tricky situation on his hands. He knows that at least one student really disliked a project that he loves, and he also recalls that in prior years, other students have expressed similar objections less emphatically, but nonetheless clearly. As he faces the possibility that he may have been too rigid, Uri uses a tried-and-true method of responding to student voice by transparently considering and addressing all concerns, even those that are difficult to hear. His process cannot work well unless students have found it to be helpful in the past; otherwise, they will not trust him. To get a better sense of how to implement this strategy, Figure 9.1 presents some key ideas around ensuring that feedback on feedback produces ideal results.

In Figure 9.1, the steps to conducting effective feedback on feedback are outlined along with a specific look into how the process plays out. Note that both individual and collective concerns are addressed in this illustration, which may seem odd at first. Why take time to talk about what only one person shared? The reason is that it's entirely possible that many students have the same question but only one feels comfortable asking it. In addition, there are times when a teacher cannot resolve

**Figure 9.1. Toolbox Timesaver: Feedback on Feedback**

**Helpful Habit:** *Make visible follow-through the primary goal of feedback on feedback.*

**Steps for Success**

1. Look for patterns in the feedback and put more emphasis on responding to what a larger number of students have expressed.
2. Respond to all feedback comments unless they are intended to be unproductive.
3. Outliers matter, but do not let them hold undue influence on future action unless they point to a clear problem that needs resolution.
4. In addition to expressing intent to make change, follow through quickly and transparently by explicitly sharing action(s) with students.
5. After each period of study, continue to gather feedback on feedback that reflects a larger learning objective (unit, marking period, etc.).

**Example:** Feedback-on-Feedback Protocol

| Student Feedback | Teacher Response |
| --- | --- |
| We're doing too much group work. I need time to think on my own. | Although we must have some group work to remain collaborative, I'll build more quiet processing time into future projects. |
| Discussions can be great, but there are so many tangents. I get distracted. | Sometimes tangents can be productive and related to what we learn. Other times they are distracting. I will be mindful of helping the class remain focused. |
| The project was a huge part of my grade, and I didn't do that well. Can I do something to fix my grade? | Parts of the project are eligible for reassessment, so please come talk to me. |

student concerns, either partially or at all. In Figure 9.1, for example, the teacher explains that although tangents during discussions can be distracting, they sometimes lead toward learning in unexpected ways. Assuming that the reason for not following a suggestion is fully explained with a clear rationale, most students will feel satisfied after hearing the feedback on feedback. Then, as teachers take into account what students have shared, they return to the process of backward design with the vital element of student voice as a guide for moving ahead.

## Back to the Beginning?

Planning effective instruction starts from an endpoint. Then, teachers work their way toward the beginning in the process known as "backward design" that we explored in Chapter 3. When backward design is executed correctly, the trajectory of instruction is guided by a central objective. Teachers then develop or identify how that objective will be measured through evidence before they plan activities for instruction. Once students have completed a designated chunk of learning, the process begins anew. But if teachers dive straight back into planning without taking some time to figure out where things stand, they may be setting themselves up for repeating some missteps.

To avoid the kind of repetition that stymies student achievement, teachers must build strong links between design and action. That way, the smaller details of adjusting instruction don't get lost in the shuffle. Figure 9.2 exemplifies one way of bringing backward design into focus with specific action steps for moving forward.

When teachers map out a unit, student voice can play a part only if they intentionally work it into the process of planning. In Figure 9.2, a 4th grade social studies class has been studying state history and is moving toward the study of topography. Before making final plans, the teacher looks at student voice data and makes adjustments that will be applied to planning in future class sessions. That way, student feedback does not go ignored. As a next step, the teacher can explicitly share with students what changes are being made for Unit 3, and why.

Once the effective execution of feedback on feedback becomes a habit, the results and benefits are highly visible. If the process of gathering student voice seems overwhelming, begin with asking for just one comment, question, or concern in relation to a learning target. As students begin to see the results of their feedback in action, and as you become more accustomed to asking for information and using it to guide practice, it will become increasingly comfortable to check in with learning during any transitional points that occur in the course of instruction.

## There Is No Such Thing as "After Instruction"

*Uri throws his arms in the air, making a "V" sign for "victory" with his fingers. "Awesome!" he says out loud.*

*"Good news?"*

## Figure 9.2. From Backward Design to Action

---

**Helpful Habit:** *Connect backward design to feedback on feedback for optimal results.*

**Unit 2 Objective**

Students will analyze and interpret both primary and secondary sources to gain a deeper understanding of state history.

**Student Feedback Summary, Unit 2**

- Some of the primary sources were difficult to understand. The vocabulary of the time period was unfamiliar.
- Certain secondary sources were identified as "boring," because they were considered to be either dry or difficult to understand.
- There were several requests for "more stories" and "fun activities."
- Generally, students appreciated their visit to the living history museum and the artifacts they encountered.

**Assessment Notes, Unit 2**

- The majority of students met the standard on the final project; those who did not were resistant to interpreting the primary sources. Perhaps there was an underlying comprehension issue?
- Some students extended beyond the stated objective by comparing the events of the time period to conflicts they have read or heard about in modern times.
- Moving forward, think about ways to make primary sources more accessible without lowering the standard.

**Design Approach, Unit 3**

**Objective**

Students will apply their knowledge of state history to the identification and description of local geography.

**Evidence of Success**

Students will be assigned a state region to study and complete a report that showcases specific features, such as bodies of water or mountains.

**Possible Activities**

- Create a plan for a city or town visit. What would you want to see? What monuments or sites are significant, and why?
- Conduct research about how people in different geographical regions live their daily lives. How does one region differ from another, and why?
- Develop a subunit on topography and reading maps (perhaps the latter as an extension?).

**Adjustments from Unit 2**

- Provide scaffolding for primary sources with vocabulary terms.
- Incorporate first-person accounts and other narrative experiences along with informational text to meet the request for "stories."
- Look at secondary sources again to ensure a variety of perspectives and approaches.
- Create an optional extension for visiting local monuments if desired in connection with the assessment.

*Startled, Uri turns to the student standing behind him. "Jackson! I didn't see you there. I'm sorry."*

*"No problem," Jackson says. "You seemed happy. I didn't want to interrupt."*

*Uri smiles at him. "You're not interrupting. I was just excited about the historical fiction project everyone turned in yesterday. The results look pretty great."*

*"Oh, awesome," Jackson says, exhaling in relief. "I was worried. I've never been able to just pick whatever I want to focus on. I kept second-guessing myself."*

*"You did great," Uri says. "And I'm glad we got a chance to do this after the children's book. I couldn't change that assignment, but I know that some people in the class wanted more freedom about how they did this next assignment. That was a great idea. Did you come to discuss your work?"*

*"Not really. I was wondering if you had a snack. I forgot my lunch."*

*Uri nods, pulling out his desk drawer. "You came to the right place. I've got these new oat bars. They're surprisingly good."*

*"You sure you don't mind? I'm not taking your snack?"*

*"Not at all," Uri says. "I always have tons. Pick a flavor."*

*As Jackson takes one, he gestures toward the stack of projects. "So now what? What happens next?"*

*"Excellent question," Uri says. "And the answer is always the same. We keep going. There's always more to learn, perhaps especially for me."*

*"Right," Jackson says. "I kind of meant more specifically."*

*Uri laughs. "I can answer that, too. But I think I need to gather more feedback on feedback first. Can you ask me again in a few days?"*

◄ ——————— ►

Although this section of the book has been titled "After Instruction," there is no such thing. Teaching is a recursive process, not to be confused with a repetitive process. With the latter, we do the same thing over and over and expect different results, and when that doesn't happen, frustration is almost unavoidable. To ensure that instruction is focused on building student capacity, think of the following "habit stacks" to make the process more meaningful:

1. When students get stuck, uncover all the possible reasons that might be happening by listening to their voices rather than creating hypotheses in isolation.
2. Examine areas of dissonance between your perceptions of student performance and their perspectives.
3. Elicit suggestions for the future frequently and with an open mind.

Recursive teaching has a reflective component that comes with productive struggle. In this model, teachers learn from what has worked and consider how mistakes lead to better outcomes in the future. With an open and curious mindset, the idea is to return to the first stages of planning instruction with more perspective, clarity, and information.

**Tiny Teaching Tips: Next Steps**

"Feedback is key. It is also wasted unless you provide class time for students to apply it to their work."

*—Ryan Love, high school English teacher*

"I try to slow myself down a little bit before finishing one unit and starting the next. I need that processing time, or the decisions I make might not be the best ones."

*—2nd grade teacher*

# IV

# WELL-BEING AND BELONGING

The bulk of this book has been devoted to the topic of building small habits that maximize results for both teachers and students in the stages that occur before, during, and after instruction. However, it would be remiss to ignore two very important aspects of how individuals can enter and remain in an ideal headspace to accomplish their best work: well-being and belonging. When we're not well, be it physically or emotionally, the ability to do our best work is severely compromised. In addition, feeling alienated or isolated in a school community can stymie any possible progress.

For that reason, taking some time toward the close of this book to denote habits for wellness brings home a foundational truth about teaching: it is about people. That is why, despite as much content knowledge as teachers may possess, they cannot be effective in the classroom until they recognize the irrefutable fact that they aren't just there to teach a class—they're there to teach students. Kids need adults to step up and keep themselves well.

In terms of student wellness, one of the many beautiful aspects of teaching lies in the continuous opportunity to adjust our approach and develop fresh pathways to learning. When we create even better experiences for students, it is not only their academic experiences that are enhanced; their well-being and sense of belonging also benefit from the support of teachers who care about them. As we build habits around the before, during, and after of instruction itself, we are also developing equally effective practices that support overall wellness throughout the school community.

# 10

# Teacher and Student Well-being

*Tara is barely making it. She was up late into the night finishing paperwork for her students with accommodations, and kids have been pushing her buttons all day.*

*Looking back, she realizes that she never should have let her administrator give her four different preps. Tara was trying to be helpful by saying yes, but teaching so many different grade levels in the course of one day is just too much. Lately, the burnout has been relentless.*

*Tara glances at the clock on her classroom wall and sees that it is nearly 3:30. She has been staring at the same student work for the past half hour and can't seem to focus enough to finish grading even one more paper.* Time to throw in the towel for an hour or two, *she thinks, putting the papers in her bag to take home.*

*As Tara digs through her bag to find the car keys, her email lets out a ping. Reflexively, Tara clicks on the message without stopping to consider whether she should just leave it for now.*

*She reads through the email and feels rage bubbling up. It's from the head of the special education department, letting Tara know that there is a new attached form to fill out for each of her students. Although the message is apologetic, she asks that Tara complete the paperwork by close of business the next day.*

*Tara's hands hover over the keyboard, shaking. She wants to write back with a flood of indignation. How can this person expect her to spend another sleepless night doing yet more work, and with absolutely no notice? Her papers sit ungraded, her lessons unplanned, and all she wants is an hour or two to get something to eat and use the bathroom.*

*Her fingers remain suspended, frozen over her laptop. Tara realizes that as much as she wants to unleash a piece of her mind, it won't do any good.* My fault for never saying no, *she thinks as she sits back down, clicking on the attachment and putting down her bag.*

# Teacher Wellness: Taking Care of You

Despite best intentions, a day in the life of a teacher can spiral out of control quickly. People get in the habit of working through each day, making themselves available at all times, without getting a break or proper nutrition and putting personal needs last no matter how run-down they might feel. To counteract behavior that can only lead to burnout if it remains unchecked, it's crucial to take steps toward changes that will provide some much-needed space from an otherwise relentless focus on work.

Taking large strides toward change is nearly impossible in terms of both starting and maintaining different habits. Instead, small moments can have a huge impact on wellness without sacrificing too much time. Even better, these little moves can be stacked on top of one another over time to produce a more adaptive shift. To get the ball rolling, here is a list of short wellness "snacks" that can occur either during school hours or outside the duty day:

- Go outside the building, either to take a walk or to sit on a bench and just focus on the world outside. If desired, bring along a colleague for a social chat.
- Bring a puzzle to work (Sudoku, crossword, Wordle) and set aside time to be alone and complete it.
- Meditate (using an app, if desired) in any space that will remain undisturbed.

- Take several minutes to mindfully enjoy a special snack without having your phone or any distractions nearby.
- At lunch, chat with colleagues about their lives or a favorite TV show, but resist talking shop.
- Take a stretch break or use a foam roller to relax the muscle kinks that occur from the active work of teaching.
- Pick an activity to calm your mind (doodling, knitting, listening to music) and give yourself the time to engage in this activity without any other distractions.
- If a private space is available, set a timer for a brief power nap or just a quiet rest.
- Have a phone conversation with a friend or loved one who keeps you grounded or affirms you.
- Take some time to journal, writing personal thoughts and affirmations or just whatever pops into your head.
- Make or buy a hot drink and slowly enjoy it without letting distractions (such as other people or sudden demands) get in the way.

To make these wellness "snacks" more powerful, think about how to gradually build upon a smaller habit. Doing so might include increasing the time spent on a break from 15 minutes to 30 on days that are lighter, or adding more of the wellness actions to your daily or weekly repertoire. Although gradually taking on smaller habits might not be the huge shift you are seeking, doing anything at all (and eventually taking on additional healthy moves) is far more attainable and produces better results than doing nothing. Once some better habits become ingrained, it also becomes far easier to turn attention back to the important goal of helping *students* feel their best and focus on their work.

# Student Wellness: Taking Care of Kids

Anyone who works with children knows all too well from the reverberations of the pandemic that many kids are not all right, but the reasons why remain unclear—at least to a certain degree. In terms of providing help with social-emotional learning (SEL), teachers might feel a little lost when it comes to providing support to students; after all, being trained in curriculum and instruction does not always translate to feeling confident about resolving issues that fall more under the umbrella of school counseling or psychology practice. Unfortunately, the result of that gap in expertise for teachers can result in a situation where in a majority of classes, according to author and trauma-informed education expert Alex Shevrin Venet, "there is no time where teachers connect directly with students at all."

Teachers are better equipped to help students than they realize, even if that means connecting a struggling child to someone with more expertise. Phyllis Fagell, a licensed clinical professional counselor, certified professional school counselor, and author, recommends letting kids know that they are not alone and telling them, "If you need support, I'm a helper. If I'm not equipped to get you support, I will be the bridge to help you get that support." Just as students must be encouraged to tap into the growth-mindset behavior of asking for help when needed by pulling from available resources, teachers must model the same process when an issue arises that may feel beyond the purview of classroom instruction.

Another important conversation teachers can have with students early in the year is to help them understand their feelings and to be open about what it means to be bogged down in work as opposed to experiencing something that needs the help of a school counselor. Fagell offers this recommendation: "Take a minute to define anxiety and depression to help kids know the difference between those two terms and understand them. Sometimes, when kids think they are experiencing anxiety, it could also be they are overwhelmed or disorganized." Paying attention to the nature of the problem, especially for students who are transitioning to a new school or moving from primary to secondary grades, can help to pinpoint exactly what wellness moves are best.

When students struggle to achieve content goals because they are too distracted, overwhelmed, or otherwise unwell from a mental health perspective, teachers can use several small but significant ways to model practices that connect wellness to learning. Various ideas about how to connect wellness to learning lie well within the teacher's scope of expertise and can make significant strides toward helping students achieve a calm and productive mindset while in class. Here are some examples:

- Be explicit and consistent with providing messages that communicate caring—for example, "You and your success are important to me."
- When students make contributions to class, validate them by celebrating responses (especially incorrect ones) as pathways to learning.
- Resist putting kids on the spot or "cold calling." Instead, give them time, space, or the option to talk to a friend before sharing thoughts with the class.
- Do not grade students for participation. Doing so sends a message to less vocal students that they are not valued, confuses understanding of the purpose of grades, and sows the seeds of distrust.
- Provide varied ways for all students to have their voices heard in class.
- To give students a way to share that sometimes they may need extra help focusing, agree ahead of time on a method of communication.
- Take time to focus on individual students throughout the week by being intentional about a quick check-in, even for a minute or two. If needed, make a rotation list as a reminder of who has not been checked on recently.
- Strive toward establishing deeper conversations by starting with lower-risk, accessible topics and gradually increasing the focus on profound, critical thinking.

Although this list shares some starting points, teachers may be out of their depth at times with managing student wellness and therefore may need to collaborate with other experts within the building, such as school psychologists and counselors. However, that doesn't mean that all matters connected to SEL fall outside classroom walls. As Fagell affirms, "So much of kids' mental health challenges come down to logistical and social issues that teachers can address." By building the trust that keeps lines of communication open and listening carefully to kids when they talk about their challenges, teachers can make the important judgment call of determining which issues they can resolve.

When in doubt, adults should never hesitate to reach out for help. Shevrin Venet agrees that teachers are not expected to be the only resource for children in the building: "It's not your job to carry a student through their whole healing and wellness journey; it's your job to be the coordinator to people who can do that work." The job of a teacher is not to know everything; it is to model how to reach out and get the best information possible. Furthermore, showing students that little actions throughout their school day can have a positive impact on their overall focus and sense of well-being is yet another victory that moves kids beyond transient external motivators and toward long-term, sustainable habits.

# Habit Stacking for Wellness

*"How's everything going?" Ms. Carlton asks David, who is working in her classroom at lunchtime. "Feeling OK these days?"*

*David looks up from his laptop and smiles at her. "Yeah, everything is fine. I'm sorry I was such a pain last week."*

*"Don't be sorry. If you hadn't told me you were struggling, we wouldn't have figured out how to make things better."*

*"I guess," David says. "But sometimes I'm still frustrated by my own anxiety. It's not as bad these days, but it's still something I have to pay attention to. Like yesterday, I'd done my math homework and it was ready to turn in, and I almost didn't give it to my teacher because I was so worried that it was completely wrong."*

*"But you did give it to her, right?" Ms. Carlton asks.*

*"I did. But you know, I'm mad that I even thought about not doing it."*

*Ms. Carlton shakes her head. "You're focused on the wrong part here. Listen, it might be hard to manage your inner voice sometimes, the one that tells you that your work isn't good enough. But you know what? Yesterday, you won. You didn't listen to that voice, and you turned in your work. Don't you see how great that is?"*

*"I do," David acknowledges. "I just wish that voice would go away completely."*

*"It might, or it might not. And that's something to keep talking to your school counselor about. But for now, having strategies to cope with it is major progress. I'm really proud of you, David."*

*"Thanks." David smiles at Ms. Carlton and turns his attention back to his laptop to get his work done.*

Students like David are not rare. They come to class, work hard, and pay attention. However, their fear of being "less than" can wind up projecting outward in a way that is deceiving. Teachers may assume that certain students are lazy or uncaring when, in fact, their feelings of inadequacy and intimidation prevent them from showing teachers or fellow students the work they have completed. Therefore, any adult in the classroom should be aware of how difficult it can be to risk sharing ideas or work with a large group, and to make learning spaces as safe as possible.

To normalize the fact that everyone gets nervous, teachers can build habitual practices for helping students manage their anxiety in ways that gather power over time. For example, Phyllis Fagell recommends a strategy known as the "Coping Jar." When students identify an effective coping mechanism they like to use, they write their idea on one side of a popsicle stick and explain when or how they use it on the other side. Teachers can also participate in creating this classroom resource. When anyone in the class has a difficult moment, they can go to the jar and see if there's a stick with a strategy that can help them. This method is a simple but powerful way for the class to collaboratively take responsibility for helping one another as, one popsicle stick after another, students build the habit of recognizing and supporting measures that increase their ability to cope with stress.

Along similar lines, Shevrin Venet recommends conducting regular check-ins with kids via a number of possible methods, such as an online form, sticky notes, greetings at the doorway, or restorative circles, which is a discussion technique focused on either building or repairing relationships. Taking small moments throughout any given school week to make sure that each student is OK sends the important message that everyone in the room has value. Once students believe that teachers have their backs, they will be more likely to open themselves to stacking strong academic habits with incremental support. Figure 10.1 offers some examples of how to tie the act of changing behavior to making progress in class. The idea behind the examples in Figure 10.1 is to transparently show students that getting better is a gradual process. This more measured approach to progress can be tailored to individuals or applied to the whole class. For example, as Fagell recommends, "Spend five minutes a day having kids pull out calendars and decide what they have to do together." When students see that being organized is something lots of people struggle with, they will not feel as self-conscious about reaching out when workloads begin to feel like too much.

In addition, teachers can adopt a habit-stacking mindset to create the kinds of connections with students that allow for greater risk taking. Shevrin Venet advises, "Stop thinking of relationship building as activities in the first week of school. Instead, build wellness into every day." Consistency will always be more effective than sporadic attention to reaching goals, and students who see teachers making regular efforts to include them in a classroom community will be far more likely to feel comfortable and to think that they belong.

**Figure 10.1.  Habit-Stack Progression**

| **Helpful Habit:** *Teach students how to build gradual habits for success.* | | |
|---|---|---|
| **Habit #1:**<br>**Do my homework.** | **Habit #2:**<br>**Organize my binders.** | **Habit #3:**<br>**Ask for help.** |
| Write down one assignment each day for a few days. | Take all my papers out of their binders. | Pick a class I need the most help in. |
| Do the assignment I picked to write down, and ask my dad to check my work. | Sort the papers by subject, and make sure I have folders for each one. | Draft an email to the teacher asking for help, and ask someone I trust to look at it. |
| Write down a second assignment in my notebook. | Organize my papers for just one subject. | Send the email to the teacher. |

**Tiny Teaching Tips: Teacher and Student Well-being**

"Use reflection moments to extend metacognition beyond what's working in class to also have students reflect on wellness."

—*Alex Shevrin Venet, author and educator*

"Designate an object students can put on their desks that signals they need support."

—*Phyllis Fagell, licensed clinical professional counselor, certified professional school counselor, and author*

# Belonging

Even if all the pieces are in place for well-being, everything can wind up derailing when kids or adults don't feel like they belong. Schools are inherently cliquey if nobody takes steps to mitigate that tendency, and those who sit on the outskirts wind up feeling disenfranchised. This feeling is pervasive across all age groups and regardless of what a person's role might be. Sometimes the reasons that people feel this lack of belonging are clear, but often they remain elusive and difficult to address openly.

However, regardless of why people feel alienated from a learning community, schools cannot accept the fact that some people are outside the circle. For adults, the responsibility falls on school leaders to check in on teachers fairly regularly. Beyond typical staff appreciation lunches or classroom observation conferences, the relationships between administrators and teachers need to be built on mutual respect and a consistent effort to get to know one another. Doing so could be as simple as school leaders being more visible in the hallways to engage in casual conversations or spending more time in teacher team rooms. When leaders immerse themselves more in the spaces that teachers inhabit rather than cloistering themselves in offices, they are more likely to see who might be existing on the fringes and make more efforts to be welcoming.

For students, teachers can implement a gradual approach to creating a sense of belonging that produces results over time. Resisting the urge to move too quickly is paramount. As Alex Shevrin Venet points out, "Teachers want students to share things about themselves, but you can't jump to that. It's how you build the safety for vulnerability by making opportunities for students' literal voices to be present each day or week." Doing so might look like starting the year by asking students safer questions about things like favorite animals or ice cream flavors and then incrementally progressing to deeper topics of conversation.

At any age and stage, people need to feel as though they have a place in the world they inhabit. When teachers and students are unwell or feel separated from those around them, the important work of instruction cannot proceed with any kind of functionality. Simply put, we need to be healthy in every possible way to make space for learning. To feel more connected to the communities you inhabit, consider these habit-driven tips for success:

- Join educator groups that meet outside school, such as advocacy organizations that work to promote equity for all teachers and students.
- Find a way to contribute to the school community after hours, such as helping with a theater production or attending events that your students organize or participate in.
- Spend some time in the geographical area in which you work exploring local landmarks or getting to know the culture and vibe.
- Think about ways to connect positively to colleagues that do not involve discussing work, such as joining a regular happy hour or becoming part of a group that shares a common outside interest.
- Take intentional time each day to leave the classroom and walk around to avoid becoming isolated, whether that means heading into a team space or engaging with people in the hallways.
- Reach out to a trusted colleague for support when burnout and stress threaten to become overwhelming.

Like teaching and learning itself, staying connected to others and ourselves is a gradual process driven by habits we build intentionally over time. Throughout this book, the power of small and mighty moves for success has been prioritized over larger adaptations in process or behavior as the best pathway forward not just for school improvement, but also for the lives of those who occupy school buildings each day. Just as we don't expect to lift a barbell and suddenly get stronger the next day, becoming more skillful as educators is a process that occurs slowly but surely with the right intention. When we take those first steps toward stacking habits for success, the results that follow as academic growth and well-being align are nothing short of miraculous.

## Tiny Teaching Tip: Belonging

"Students need to see schools and classrooms as places they belong, see themselves in the content that is taught, and feel respected as their fully authentic, racial, and ethnic selves."

—*Charles Alexander, instructional specialist*

# References

American Psychological Association. (2018). Cognitive overload. *APA Dictionary*. Author. https://dictionary.apa.org/cognitive-overload

Barshay, J. (2022). Researchers blast data analysis for teachers to help students. *Hechinger Report*. https://hechingerreport.org/proof-points-researchers -blast-data-analysis-for-teachers-to-help-students/

Chappuis, S., & Chappuis, J. (2012). The best value in formative assessment. ASCD. https://pdo.ascd.org/lmscourses/PD13OC001/media/Leadership_Implementing -the-CCCSS_Module3_Reading1.pdf

Cineas, F. (2022). Are teachers leaving the classroom en masse? *Vox*. https://www .vox.com/policy-and-politics/2022/8/18/23298916/teacher-shortages-debate -local-national

Clear, J. (2018). *Atomic habits: An easy and proven way to build good habits and break bad ones*. Avery.

Fredricks, J. A., Blumenfeld, P. C., & Paris, A. H. (2004). School engagement: Potential of the concept, state of the evidence. *Review of Educational Research, 74*(1), 59–109.

Friend, M., & Cook, L. (2009). *Interactions: Collaboration skills for school professionals* (6th ed.). Pearson.

Greenberg, J., Putman, H., & Walsh, K. (2014). *Training our future teachers: Classroom management*. National Council on Teacher Quality. https://www.nctq.org/ dmsView/Future_Teachers_Classroom_Management_NCTQ_Report

Janis, I. L. (1982). *Groupthink: Psychological studies of policy decisions and fiascoes* (2nd ed.). Cengage Learning.

Jha, A. (2020). The brain science of attention and overwhelm. *Mindful*. https://www .mindful.org/youre-overwhelmed-and-its-not-your-fault/

Kaplan, M. (2012). Collaborative team teaching: Challenges and rewards. *Edutopia*. https://www.edutopia.org/blog/collaborative-team-teaching-challenges -rewards-marisa-kaplan

Kois, D. (2023). An interview with the school board chair who forced out a principal after Michelangelo's *David* was shown in class. *Slate*. https://slate.com/human -interest/2023/03/florida-principal-fired-michelangelo-david-statue.html

Luca, M. (2021). Leaders: Stop confusing correlation with causation. *Harvard Business Review*. https://hbr.org/2021/11/leaders-stop-confusing-correlation-with -causation

McCormack, J. (2014). *Brief: Make a bigger impact by saying less*. Wiley.

Mofield, E. L. (2020). Benefits and barriers to collaboration and co-teaching: Examining perspectives of gifted education teachers and general education teachers. *Gifted Child Today, 43*(1), 20–33. https://journals.sagepub.com/doi/full/10.1177/1076217519880588

Plotinsky, M. (2022). *Teach more, hover less: How to stop micromanaging your secondary classroom*. W. W. Norton.

Rosenthal, R., & Jacobson, L. (1968). Pygmalion in the classroom. *The Urban Review, 3*, 16–20. https://sites.tufts.edu/tuftsliteracycorps/files/2017/02/Pygmalion -in-the-Classroom.pdf

Saphier, J., Haley-Speca, M. A., & Gower, R. (2018). *The skillful teacher: The comprehensive resource for improving teaching and learning* (7th ed.). Research for Better Teaching.

Schleifer, D., Rinehart, C., & Yanisch, T. (2017). *Teacher collaboration in perspective: A guide to research*. Public Agenda. https://files.eric.ed.gov/fulltext/ED591332.pdf

Venables, D. R. (2014). *How teachers can turn data into action*. ASCD.

Wiggins, G. (2012). Seven keys to effective feedback. *Educational Leadership, 70*(1). https://www.ascd.org/el/articles/seven-keys-to-effective-feedback

Wiggins, G., & McTighe, J. (2005). *Understanding by design* (2nd ed.). ASCD.

# Index

# About the Author

 **Miriam Plotinsky** is an instructional specialist with Montgomery County Public Schools in Maryland, where she has taught and led for more than 20 years. She is the author of three books for educators: *Teach More, Hover Less: How to Stop Micromanaging Your Secondary Classroom; Lead Like a Teacher: How to Elevate Expertise in Your School;* and *Writing Their Future Selves: Instructional Strategies to Affirm Student Identity.* Miriam is a regular contributor to several publications, including *Education Week* and *Edutopia,* and she is a frequent guest on education podcasts internationally. Also a National Board–certified teacher with additional certification in administration and supervision, she lives in Silver Spring, Maryland.

## Related ASCD Resources

At the time of publication, the following resources were available (ASCD stock numbers appear in parentheses).

*Building Educator Capacity Through Microcredentials* by Eric M. Carbaugh, Laura McCullough, Meghan Raftery, and Ebbie Linaburg (#123013)

*Educator Bandwidth: How to Reclaim Your Energy, Passion, and Time* by Jane Kise and Ann Holm (#122019)

*Highly Effective PLCs and Teacher Teams* (Quick Reference Guide for Leaders) by Steve Ventura and Michelle Ventura (#QRG123050)

*Illuminate the Way: The School Leader's Guide to Addressing and Preventing Teacher Burnout* by Chase Mielke (#123032)

*Make Teaching Sustainable: Six Shifts That Teachers Want and Students Need* by Paul Emerich France (#123011)

*The Minimalist Teacher* by Tamera Musiowsky-Borneman and C. Y. Arnold (#121058)

*Rekindle Your Professional Fire: Powerful Habits for Becoming a More Well-Balanced Teacher* by Mike Anderson (#124027)

*Small Shifts, Meaningful Improvement: Collective Leadership Strategies for Schools and Districts* by P. Ann Byrd, Alesha Daughtrey, Jonathan Eckert, and Lori Nazareno (#123007)

*Still Learning: Strengthening Professional and Organizational Capacity* by Allison Rodman (#121034)

*Streamlining the Curriculum: Using the Storyboard Approach to Frame Compelling Learning Journeys* by Heidi Hayes Jacobs and Allison Zmuda (#123020)

*Teaching with Clarity: How to Prioritize and Do Less So Students Understand More* by Tony Frontier (#121015)

*What Can I Take Off Your Plate? A Structural—and Sustainable—Approach to Countering Teacher Burnout* by Jill Handley and Lara Donnelly (#125002)

For up-to-date information about ASCD resources, go to **www.ascd.org**. You can search the complete archives of *Educational Leadership* at **www.ascd.org/el**. To contact us, send an email to member@ascd.org or call 1-800-933-2723 or 703-578-9600.